Perhaps it's not about *how* we change spiritually, but *where and when* we change that matters most. The genius of *FaultLines* is in showing where and when God shows up. Steve's gripping pastoral stories and his depth of thought about the grace of God help us clearly see the spiritually subterranean weak points where Jesus Christ shifts our souls. Steve's prophetic voice rings true in it, and it prepares the way for the next tremor that Christ will not only help me cope with, but cause me to grow through.

—DAVID DRURY, Chief of Staff to General Superintendent of The Wesleyan Church, author and coauthor of six books, including *Being Dad*, *Ageless Faith*, and *SoulShift*

Steve DeNeff helps us understand that much (perhaps most) of our spiritual growth can't be about merely learning what is programmed or scheduled by the church, curriculum, or even a preaching series like this one. Instead, it is about how most spiritual growth comes out of life itself and the hundreds of things that life sends our way. We grow as we *respond* to these things. Thus DeNeff helps us see that our "curriculum" (in teaching or preaching) is preparation—it helps us pre-decide how we intend to respond when we face these FaultLines crises in life.

—KEITH DRURY, author of *Soul Shaper*, *Common Ground*, and *Holiness for Ordinary People*; professor emeritus, Indiana Wesleyan University

No one knows how he or she will respond when the ground they are standing on becomes a high rise or a sink hole. The fact is, we base our lives and our walk with Christ way too much on our surrounding circumstances. We base our Christian walk on feelings more than on a deep faith. Who will you be when you succeed? Will you know who and whose you are when your world is smashed to smithereens? All of us will face situations when we find out if we believe in Jesus like we say we do, or not. *FaultLines* will challenge your views on Christ's blessings when things seem great. It will confirm your beliefs when your world crumbles around you, even when you face death. It may well be that the preparation for an earthquake will save us more than trying to deal with it the moment everything breaks loose.

—JIM DUNN, executive director, Church Multiplication and Discipleship, The Wesleyan Church

There are hundreds of books that invite us to a better life—often promising success, peace, and greater self-worth. However, many of the suggestions in our "feel good" culture skip over seasons of life that aren't easy, peaceful, or anything like what we imagined. In *FaultLines*, Steve DeNeff shines a light on these unavoidable moments—and these at times intense circumstances, humbly guiding us through these moments when life is difficult and scary—encouraging us to grasp onto the reality that God's love can shape us through the FaultLine. *FaultLines* presents a sound model for trusting God in the midst of hardship, and is packed with nuggets for a long journey with Jesus.

—GREG HASELOFF, associate dean of campus ministries and campus chaplain, Asbury University, Wilmore, KY

In *FaultLines*, DeNeff provides completion to the holiness equation he so powerfully defined for us in *SoulShift*: the greatest transformational shifts that God will bring about in a soul are where the most difficult and painful cracks of life run deepest. When fault lines reach down into your life (and they will), will they make your faith, or break it? A must-read for deeper disciples.

—CAP. CAROL LEWIS, Salvation Army

For too long the church has thought that the best way to make disciples was to help them, at all costs, avoid the FaultLines of life. Steve DeNeff exposes with grace the error of our thinking and leads us toward a better way of making disciples. Saints are made not beyond or above but upon the FaultLines of life. Paradoxically, the stuff we are tempted to run from actually has the potential to make us who God created us to be. *FaultLines* presents a fresh, biblical, and much-needed approach to discipleship for the twenty-first-century church.

—LENNY LUCHETTI, author of *Preaching Essentials*, associate professor of proclamation and Christian ministry, Wesley Seminary at Indiana Wesleyan University

Trusting in God's plan for our lives is easy when it looks the way we want it to. In *FaultLines*, DeNeff shares with us how to survive the unexpected shifts in our lives that can change everything. Whether it be hardship or joy, God alone can shift souls for his glory. *FaultLines* is a guide for all believers—both new and old—to be prepared for these moments of great change.

—JO ANNE LYON, General Superintendent, The Wesleyan Church

In *FaultLines*, we discover that the precise place that the Spirit-enabled transformation occurs is our very lives. We now see that these life-events themselves become our spiritual teacher and should not be seen as a distraction or as the result of moral failure. Thus, *FaultLines* is a refreshing approach at how a life focused on Jesus encounters seismic jolts which wonderfully help us to interpret Christ's desire to shape us into his image. A "fault" is not only something that happen *to* us, but a spiritual game-changer *for* us.

—DAVID SMITH, vice president for academic affairs, Kingswood University

Steve DeNeff offers a unique contribution to the subject of how to live well. This is truly a full-view and whole-life approach to maturing as a Christian. *FaultLines* manages to weave together the whole human experience as it commonly comes to most of us—good and bad—into a tapestry ready-made for God's shaping influence. It is not another book on holiness or discipleship. It is a book that incorporates both. It is thoroughly biblical and practical in its perspective on reality and our best way to respond to it. This is a read-slowly, read-with-others and read-again book.

—MATTHEW A. THOMAS, bishop, Free Methodist Church USA

Steve DeNeff is an outstanding communicator. Whether speaking from a platform or from the pages of his writings, he addresses life issues in a practical, thought-provoking, and spiritually uplifting way. I guarantee you will be personally enriched by Steve's latest book, *FaultLines: Challenges That Transform Your Soul*. It is a refreshing call for the church to reclaim its emphasis on holy living. And it's a relevant call to those at the edge of a crisis point in life to discover the joy of surrender to God's transforming power.

—STAN TOLER, speaker and author of *ReThink Your Life*, *Give to Live*, and *Total Quality Life*

FaultLines by Steve DeNeff is a rich and profound exploration of practical holiness. How is our sanctification reflected during life's difficult transitions and defining moments? This is where the rubber meets the road—an excellent guide for serious seekers of the deeper life.

—MARK O. WILSON, author of *Purple Fish* and *Filled Up, Poured Out*; senior pastor of Hayward Wesleyan Church, Hayward, WI

FAULTLiNES

challenges that transform your soul

STEVE DeNEFF

wesleyan
PUBLISHING HOUSE
wphstore.com

Copyright © 2014 by Steve DeNeff
Published by Wesleyan Publishing House
Indianapolis, Indiana 46250
Printed in the United States of America
ISBN: 978-0-89827-926-9
ISBN (e-book): 978-0-89827-927-6

Library of Congress Cataloging-in-Publication Data

DeNeff, Steve.
  FaultLines : challenges that transform your soul / Steve DeNeff.
     pages cm
  Includes bibliographical references.
  ISBN 978-0-89827-926-9 (pbk.)
  1. Spiritual formation. 2. Christian life. 3. Suffering--Religious aspects--Christianity.
  I. Title. II. Title: Fault Lines.
  BV4509.5.D457 2014
  248.4--dc23
                              2014015969

For the people of College Wesleyan Church

CONTENTS

Free discipleship resources are available for download at
www.wphresources.com/faultlines.

INTRODUCTION

Some years ago I picked up a copy of John Oswalt's little book, *Called to Be Holy*, and as I sat down to read it I could not get past the first sentence: "The fate of the Christian church around the world depends upon what the Church does with the idea of holiness."[1]

That's quite a claim.

At first, we can forgive Oswalt for making it because, after all, he's a holiness guy and that was a book on holiness. He's supposed to say things like that. But Oswalt was not just making a case for holiness. He was arguing against the pervasive shallowness of the church he continues.

Unless Christians are truly transformed into the character of God, the whole purpose of the Church's existence becomes blurred and confused. The world looks upon (the unconverted) who nevertheless claim to be the people of God and they say, "You lie!" But beyond that, a Church without the character of God lacks the power of God and we find ourselves right back in the situation that Israel was in when Isaiah told her, "You were with child and you writhed in pain, but you gave birth to wind; you did not bring salvation to the earth; you have not given birth to the people of the world."[2]

The Christian church in America is struggling to remain relevant today. The percentage of self-identified Christians has fallen ten points in the past two decades.[3] The number of unaffiliated (or "nones") has doubled to 16 percent in the past few years and most researchers think that this is not because they haven't decided which church to attend, but because they have largely written it off altogether. The number of those who think religion "can answer all or most of today's problems" has declined to an all-time low of 48 percent when, for the last twenty years, that number has never been lower than 58 percent. When asked what they would do if they needed spiritual direction, most young adults (ages 18–29) said they would read an inspirational book. Remarkably, only one in six said they would call a church.

"The Christian God isn't dead," boasted *Newsweek* magazine, "but he's less a force . . . than at any other time in recent memory."[4] In his place has come a rising number of gods from other religions or from no religion at all.[5] One in four American adults say that they attend religious services of a faith that is different from their own.

Greg Smith, senior researcher for the Pew Forum on Religion and Public Life, says that there is "a remarkable openness" among many who participate in rituals that contradict their professed faith.[6]

Even among the so-called devout, there is a general disconnect of one's ethical practices from their religious beliefs. Study after study reveals a growing number of "Christians" who are being discipled by the media or culture. Princeton researcher, Kenda Dean has labeled it a "moral therapeutic deism," which "offers comfort, bolsters self-esteem, helps solve problems, and lubricates relationships by encouraging people to do good, feel good, and keep God at arm's length."[7]

The irony in all of this is that it is happening at a time when there is more discipleship material available to the average reader than at any other time in the history of the church. Does that bother you? Let me put it more succinctly: Why is it that, with all of this discipleship material at our fingertips, we have failed to produce more and better disciples?

The short answer, I think, is that the contemporary discipleship movement (which began nearly forty years ago) has largely neglected the message of holiness. We have not been calling for holiness outcomes and we have not been offering the Holy Spirit's power to bring them about. Most of our discipleship has been about behavioral changes and not about the deep religious affections that make these changes possible.

Hannah More wrote of a sporadic religion "that is too sincere to be hypocrisy and yet too sporadic to be profitable." She went on to say:

It is too superficial to reach the heart and too unproductive to proceed from it. It is slight, but not false. It has discernment enough to distinguish sin but not firmness enough to resist it. It has enough feeling to soften the heart, but not enough courage to reform it. It weeps whenever it does wrong, and performs all of the functions of repentance for sin except forsaking it. It has everything of devotion, except stability and gives everything to its faith, except the heart. It is a spirituality of times, circumstances and events. I mean, it is brought into play by those circumstances and then dwindles away with the occasion that called it out.[8]

All of this to say that I think Oswalt was right. What is needed in our day is a renewal of Christian faith to believe in the supernatural again, and a revival of courage to make commitments and to keep them, to order our lives according to the faith that we profess.

Some years ago, I argued that we were at the crossroads between mediocrity and holiness and that we will make a serious mistake if we believe that revival will save us.[9] Oddly enough, I find myself hoping for revival nonetheless. But if it comes, it will not come as it did before. It will not come through our attempt to foster revival but through a renewed emphasis upon the spiritual formation of those in the church who are already "saved." In other words, it will come when the already-saved get converted.

Holiness writer Gordon Smith has suggested that this renewal must embrace three things: (1) a thorough and radical conversion; (2) a clear and well-articulated goal of what transformation really means; and (3) an intentional program, or model, for getting us there.[10]

In an earlier book called *SoulShift*, Dave Drury and I attempted to outline seven fundamental changes that occur in every transformed life. It was a picture of what transformation really means. We tried to show that discipleship is not a matter of learning to act one way instead of another—though actions are vitally important in this life, and even more important for the next. Rather, discipleship is a matter of learning to live in the only way that works, to do it instinctively—that is, without trying—and to do it all of the time. For this to happen, a person would have to be completely rewired, which, of course, is what *SoulShift* was about.

But why does that happen for some and not for others? Why does the discipleship process, even when it involves the message of holiness, fail to transform so many? I got my answer one afternoon while I was taking calls on a radio program. Kathy was a single mom from North Carolina, on her way to work, when she called.

"All this talk about transformation sounds very good," she said, "but I don't have time for it." What did she mean?

"Three years ago my husband left me for someone he met on the Internet, leaving me with our two children. So I turned to the church and they were a great support. I looked forward to going every week. They gave me life. Then six months ago, I lost my job and had to move to a new city where I didn't know anyone. Now, six months later, I'm working two jobs and I still don't know anyone. I can't find a good church and even if I did I wouldn't be able to attend much, because my schedule is too crazy and I'm too exhausted by the end of the week."

"I'm so sorry," I said. "Please don't be too hard on yourself in this season. What you're doing every day is heroic."

"I want to grow," she said, "but I just can't. In your book, you told us to choose a couple of shifts to work on, to find a coach and to build some disciplines into our lives. I don't have time for that. So how do you grow when you don't have time to grow?"

"What if you didn't choose two shifts or two disciplines," I countered. "What if you let the shifts choose you?"

"What do you mean?"

"Well, sometimes we think of discipleship as a series of lessons to be learned alongside whatever else is happening in our lives. It's like we have these lessons and then we have our real lives. We keep trying to get our lives to look like the curriculum. But what if our lives *are* the curriculum? What if the only thing you're supposed to learn in this season of your life is whatever it takes for you to survive this season of your life? What if you let your life, hectic as it is, be the teacher?"

"But how?" she said. "What does that look like?"

I mumbled something about being a really good mom but inside I thought to myself, "I wish I knew." This book is an attempt to answer that question.

The truth is, we have more resources than at any other time in history, but most of life falls between the answers. Most people don't grow because circumstances in their lives make it very hard for them to grow, and much of the time it isn't their fault. It's like the slogan says in the commercial for an insurance company: "Life comes at you fast!"

Discipleship, then, is not a track of lessons that runs parallel to our life. Rather, it is life itself. Discipleship is the process of aligning our real life to the outrageous claims of the gospel and coming to see that, in the end, *this* is the only life worth having. It is the only one that works. It is learning to live on earth in a way that is common sense to everyone in heaven. Even when life sets the agenda, which is most of the time, the disciple learns to ask, "What is God doing? And how do I join him in it?"

What is needed is a new vision of holiness, not as a diploma that recognizes we have met certain standards and are therefore fit to be called "holy," but as a license to practice that recognizes what God has done and gives us permission to apply this to whatever situation we are in. And what is needed is a way to interpret real life within the Christian narrative so that we're able to draw on the vast resources that await us in that narrative. Instead of asking, "How does the Bible apply to my life?" we must learn to ask, "How does my life fit into the story of the Bible? And what has God made available for me there?" One way to do that is to locate ourselves in some biblical character's story and to watch them move with God. What was God doing with him or her, or what was God doing *in* him or her, as a result of the character's circumstances?

The great boxer and eminent theologian Mike Tyson once said, "Everyone has a plan . . . until they get hit in the mouth." So this book is for those who, like Kathy, once had a plan but got hit in the mouth. It's for those who don't have time to grow. It's a kind of apology to those whose circumstances didn't fit within the church's plan for spiritual formation. And it's my apology to those, in the past, who were in extraordinary days but received from me only ordinary counsel. These gracious people have showed me that real growth is possible — indeed it is only possible — when life comes at you fast.

As with anything I write, there are those who have first written on me. These include the members of College Wesleyan Church. They hear most of my ideas long before I write them; so much of what you'll read here has their fingerprints too. These good people have lived on every one of the "FaultLines" and have modeled faith and courage there. I hope this book bears witness to the grace and beauty that God has given them. As always, I am indebted to my staff (sometimes they must wonder if I work here anymore) and especially to my executive team—Chris Williams, Judy Huffman, and Emily Vermilya—who make it possible for me to hide back here, in this office, and write. I am thankful to Alex Mandura for helping me think through the chapter on death. Alex has done more work on this subject and I hope you get to read it someday. Most of all, I am thankful for my family who has been my greatest joy and especially for my wife, Lori, who has faithfully walked with me on the FaultLines.

1

GROWING UP

When children talk about "getting big" like Daddy or Mommy, they don't mean getting older or smarter, but taller.

Maybe your family has a wall where you've marked how tall your kids were at various ages. For years, our home was a parsonage, so we used an eight-foot board I bought to mark the heights of our kids. That way, we could take it with us if we moved. As our kids grew, we noticed in them the same drive all kids have—they wanted to keep growing. They'd spot someone ahead of them on the board (usually Mom) and turn it into a competition. It seems like yesterday they were standing on their tiptoes to make their mark higher.

I still have that board, even though our kids are grown, and I pulled it out the other day to look it over. The lowest mark, at forty-two inches, was for the dog, standing on his hind legs that January day in 1998. Right above him, at fifty-five inches and growing fast, was Ashley. In the next ten months, she would grow over three inches. Pushing five feet, she was closing fast on Mom, and we heard about it every week. "When I grow up," she'd say, "I'll be taller than Mom, so I'll let her wear my old clothes." Mom enjoyed this; she loved watching her kids grow and even outgrow her. Oddly, it took Ashley two more years to catch up to her mom. After growing three inches in ten months, she added only an inch over the next two years. I got blamed for rigging it. "I'm not kidding," I told her. "Come over and look for yourself!" Then it happened. The waters parted, the heavens opened, and Ashley grew almost two inches in just five months. The board now shows a line with Ashley's name and the date: March 11, 2001. One inch below, there's a line with Mom's name and the date: "Forever!"

While Mom was cheering on our daughter, I was busy fending off our son. Men are competitive. We don't want our sons outgrowing us so young. Nick passed his mom when he was twelve and began closing in on me at sixteen. We started hearing the jokes again: "When I grow up, I'm going to dunk on Dad. I'm going to put things up so he can't reach them." Just as I thought I was about to lose my place in the family, the waters parted again, the heavens opened, and Nick slowed down. Just like that. A kid who grew almost four inches in one year couldn't grow an inch in two years. Once again, I got blamed for rigging it—and I might have been tempted—but I assure you I didn't do it. Nick topped off at just under six-foot-three on January 21, 2009.

Every child wants to grow taller. But eventually we all learn that growing taller isn't something you can work on. Most of it is hardwired into us. If you have the potential, you don't worry about it. You take care of yourself and clear the obstacles out of the way. And if you don't have it in you, there's not a lot you can do. You can only appeal to a power outside of you and ask him for a miracle.

We can't make ourselves grow, but we can get in the way. We grow because of the life in us. If we fail to learn this, we will be like the child who spots a name higher on the board and then gets frustrated at not being able to reach it. We'll start feeling stuck and bored with our lives. We'll think God has ignored us. It bears repeating, because it is so essential to our understanding of growth: We cannot make ourselves grow. We grow because of the life that is in us.

But we can hinder our growth, and we are too inclined to do it. So to grow as we've been wired to grow, we must implement practices to nourish the life that is in us.

HOW DO PEOPLE GROW?

For years I've watched people grow—really grow—and I've wondered, "What are they doing to cooperate with the life of God in them?" I've watched people shed old habits, even stubborn ones like greed, lust, or bitterness. I've seen people with angry spirits become more gracious, and people who were demanding become more patient and considerate of others. I've seen stingy people become prolific givers, shy people become visionary leaders, and loud and obnoxious people become more gracious and self-aware. And I've always wondered, "How do they do it?" We know the life in them causes them to grow. But what are they doing to cultivate that life?

So a few people on our staff began to interview them. We asked them to tell their stories and looked for patterns in what caused them to grow. And what we discovered surprised us. It was so contrary to what we were thinking and how we were organized that it caused us to reevaluate our whole plan for spiritual formation.

First, we discovered that spiritual growth for most people does not occur on a steady incline but through a series of growth spurts. People grow spiritually like they grow physically—not an inch per year, but three inches in six months and then a half inch over two years. There are seasons when they grow a lot, but most of the time they don't. And most of the time it isn't their fault. So all the classes and sermons were not causing people to grow the way we expected. They prepared people to maximize seasons of growth, but there was no direct correlation between the number of services a person attended, for example, and how much they were actually growing. Even private devotions or a daily regimen of praying did not trigger seasons of growth. Again, they helped prepare for growth, but there seemed to be no direct link between devotions, prayer, and immediate growth. Why is this?

That's another thing we learned: For most people, growth does not come from what we planned, but from managing events and circumstances that we didn't plan. In other words, we don't grow from things we make happen but from things that happen to us. Our response is what causes us to grow—or not. When our kids were growing, we always knew when a growth spurt was coming. It was preceded by two things: appetite and discomfort. They'd get so hungry they'd eat everything in the house, and they'd get really sore and irritable, complaining about pain in their knees. They were not causing their growth, they were only responding to what was happening to them.

As I look back on it now, I see the importance of teaching our children the right response to these seasons. My friend Keith Drury summarized it well when he said, "A lot of spiritual formation is a 'discipline of response,' that is, life comes at a person and when it comes our response can be one [way] or another." Spiritual growth occurs, he said, when "people are equipped in character to respond rightly to these things that come at [them]."[1]

And that was a third thing we learned: People grow more under harsh conditions than under normal conditions. Almost every person we interviewed pointed to a specific season when they grew fast, and almost everyone remembered hating it while it was happening. This isn't surprising, but it helps explain why so many people don't grow. We don't grow because, by nature, we are averse to pain. We instinctively try to avoid it, or, if we can't, get away from it as quickly as possible.

Some time ago it occurred to me that I was one of these people. Looking back on the seasons of my life when I grew the most, I noticed that I was against every one of them. Even though I would have told you I wanted to grow, I would have voted against it every time. I wasn't lying about *wanting* to grow, but I am naturally averse to pain and want to avoid it. This one discovery has changed the way I counsel people. As a minister, I was trained to help them "through" their problems. But if problems are the seasons when most people grow, maybe my role is to help them remain there long enough for growth to occur. I don't need to help them out of it. It will pass on its own. It always does. The question is what kind of person the problem will leave behind.

Which leads to the fourth thing we learned: Most people grow not from information but from interpretation. The difference between when people grow and when they don't isn't how much new information they were acquiring. Most bad decisions are made not because of a lack of information, but because of a lack of either wisdom or courage. We lack wisdom when we don't know when or how some principles apply to our lives; we don't know what we should do. And we lack courage because we don't have the muster to move forward. Neither wisdom nor courage can be developed listening to sermons, reading a book, or studying in a group. No matter how many applications a message may have, there is always some situation it doesn't seem to cover. It takes a mentor or coach to help a listener interpret what they have learned and apply it for whatever situation they are in. That meant we needed to recruit, train, and deploy a fleet of coaches to come alongside those who were struggling and help them interpret the will of God for their lives. We already had plenty of teachers who would spend one hour per week in class with thirty people. We needed interpreters who were prepared to spend thirty hours in the home with one person over the course of several months.

SHIFT HAPPENS

A few years ago, we defined spiritual transformation in terms of a "SoulShift"—one of seven fundamental changes that must take place in every believer's life, transforming us each into a new person. Each change is like an earthquake far below the surface of our lives that alters the condition of our souls and changes everything on the surface. Sometimes these shifts occur suddenly, and sometimes they take months. But they are usually confined to a season, and they are often due to forces we can't control. We said, "Shift happens!" and we were careful to pronounce it right, though I can remember at least one time when someone did not.

What we were trying to say was that too much of our spiritual growth is superficial. Too much of our discipleship is only behavior modification. It affects things on the surface but doesn't go deeper. Transformation is about God rewiring our souls until we not only do things differently, but we actually want different things. We have the "mind of Christ" (1 Cor. 2:16). That is, we are "minded like God" (see Matt. 16:23). We "participate in the divine nature" (2 Pet. 1:4). We "share in his holiness" (Heb. 12:10). All of this requires a change at the core of our being. It's not enough to act like Jesus; we have to react like him as well. It's not just establishing new habits; it's having new desires, impulses, and instincts. We said, "Imagine if every morning when you woke up, your first instinct was to do what is right, and you loved it. . . . Imagine being just as concerned about other people . . . as you were once concerned about yourself. . . . Imagine knowing the will of God so well that you don't have to ask. . . . What if you suddenly made plenty of money and you never got a raise? . . . Imagine praying twenty times as much as you do now and doing it because you like to."[2]

This kind of transformation is almost unheard of today. Even in the church, we have all but conceded that people cannot be transformed, at least not inside. We have ceased to believe in miracles. We no longer believe that God can change the nature of a thing like he changed water into wine. Most of our change takes place on the surface. It makes us nicer but not new, forgiven but not innocent. Our new gospel is devoid of mystery or miracle, and I think many people hunger for something more. They want to know, "Can God still raise the dead? Should I still hope for a miracle? Can God change me?"

I believe he can. But these changes do not occur randomly or simply because we want them to. They occur by design. Like earthquakes, these SoulShifts do not happen just anywhere. They happen over FaultLines. Fault lines are places in the earth's crust where the plates are cracked, like a concrete sidewalk, and the movement and pressure from the earth's inner core keeps jostling these plates around until two of them knock into each other. And when that happens, there are three possibilities. They move apart from each other (called a tension fault), rub alongside each other (called a strike-slip fault), or jam into each other (called a reverse fault). But you can be sure, when these interior plates knock into each other, there will be a seismic change that goes all the way up to the surface.

Though earthquakes rock the earth's surface, they are triggered much deeper, in the earth's inner core. In order to "cure" the earth of an earthquake, you would have to deal with what's happening farther down. Without settling things in the earth's inner core, you would never be able to prevent the world from having earthquakes. The planet would always be prone to them. Your best-laid plans would get disrupted again and again.

But wait a minute. Not all disruptions are bad. Fault lines don't always destroy. Sometimes they create. Yes, fault lines are responsible for volcanoes, and volcanoes always destroy. In 1980 a fault line triggered a volcano that took two thousand feet off the top of Mount Saint Helens, killing fifty-seven people and costing over one billion dollars in property damages. But fault lines can also be creative. It was a fault line that created the beautiful Victoria Falls, one of the seven natural wonders of the world.

Just as fault lines are the cause of earthquakes, I think there are spiritual FaultLines that cause SoulShifts. These are seasons of life in which we feel the movement, pressure, friction, and heat of our soul's unfinished business. We do not choose these seasons; they choose us, but these are the seasons when SoulShifts are most likely to occur. Most FaultLines are the result of a deeper restlessness in our inner core. They occur randomly, sometimes violently, and they alter everything on the surface.

In his book *Care of the Soul*, Thomas Moore says that we often compensate for our problems by developing tendencies that are opposite the problems and that, over time, these tendencies we develop become new problems themselves. "It is remarkable," says Moore, "how often people think they will be better off without the things that bother them. . . . If, as a therapist, I did what I was told I'd be taking things away from people all day long. But I don't try to eradicate problems. . . . Rather, I try to give what is problematical back to the person in a way that shows its necessity, even its value."[3]

Moore is referring to what we call a FaultLine. These are periods of great upheaval. They are always disruptive, always unfair, but not always bad. The ground beneath us is moving in one of only two ways: It will either make us better or worse. It will create in us a volcano of anxiety or a waterfall of grace. It will destroy us or create in us a supernatural wonder. In the beginning, we never know which way it will go. But we know this for sure: Things will never be the same again. They never are when we're living on a FaultLine.

ONE QUESTION, TWO CULTURES

One afternoon, Philip and Andrew told Jesus about a couple of Greeks who had come to the festival to see him. Jesus froze, as if in shock, as if he couldn't speak, lost in his thoughts. Finally, he collected himself and said, "The hour has come . . ."

What hour?

It was predetermined, something set long ago. No doubt it must have come up in those long conversations he had with the Father deep in the night. It was private. Personal. It was an appointment only he could keep. It was destiny. Fate. And this was zero hour. After this, everything would be different, and it could go either way.

"The hour has come," he said, "and now my soul is troubled."

The word *troubled* means "to shake something . . . and throw it into confusion; to disturb, to upset, to confound or to agitate."[4] It's something like a panic attack. It suggests fear, anxiety, heaviness, and violence. Jesus was in chaos. He was shaken and confused. He was fragile. It's hard to imagine the Son of God in this state of mind, because these days, we prescribe medicine for people with souls like this. One writer even translates it, "Right now my life is so deeply depressed."[5]

"My soul is troubled," he said, "and what shall I say? 'Father, save me from this hour'? No, it was for this very reason I came to this hour. Father, glorify your name" (John 12:27–28).

Every FaultLine is an hour where our souls are troubled. And the question that lies at the bottom of each is, "What shall we say?" There are only two possible answers, and each is a culture unto itself. The culture of *control* says, "Father, save me from this hour." And the culture of *trust* says, "Father, glorify your name." There are no other options. There is no middle ground. They have nothing in common. And there is not much time to decide. In our fallenness, we will almost always choose control unless we learn to practice trust.

If we go the one way, we will try to get back to normal, because normal is safe. Normal is familiar, good, fair, and right. Everybody likes normal, because normal is what we were before our soul was troubled. So getting back to normal is a good thing . . . providing we were normal to begin with. But what if we weren't? What if we weren't even born normal? What if nobody was? And what if the normal we've been trying to get back to isn't the real normal? What if never being the same again isn't a bad thing? What if the things we're afraid will wreck us are actually seasons that jar us back to the real normal? It may seem awkward at first, but if we could learn to trust God instead of taking control in these situations, we could actually become more aligned with the kingdom of God in the seasons when our souls are troubled.

Too often, we cannot. We are born with instincts to survive, to avoid discomfort, and so whenever these seasons come along, we resist them. We block them. We fix them. We explain them. We blame them. This is the way of control. But the way of trust is different. When we trust God in these seasons, we improvise. We adapt. We hold loosely to our plans.

I'm thinking of the ethicist John Kavanaugh, who visited Mother Teresa to seek advice on how to spend the rest of his life.[6] When she asked what he wanted her to pray for, Kavanaugh already knew the answer: "Pray that I have clarity."

Teresa smiled and said, "No, I will not do that. Clarity is the last thing you are clinging to and must let go of."

"But you always seem to have such clarity," he said.

This time she laughed. "I have never had clarity, but I have always had trust. So I will pray that you learn to trust."

Brennan Manning wrote, "The way of trust is a movement into obscurity, into the undefined, into ambiguity, and not into some predetermined and clearly delineated plan for our future. [When we trust], the next step discloses itself only out of a discernment that God is acting in the desert of the present moment."[7]

Trust is the only way to survive on a FaultLine. If we resist, we will try to control the outcome. When it becomes apparent that we cannot, we will get stuck and resent God for leaving us there. We will complain that life is unfair. We will wonder, as Job's wife did, why we still bother with integrity. But if we can trust when it feels more natural to control, we will become resilient and optimistic about the future, even though we can't see it. But our confidence will not proceed from our own resourcefulness. It will come from the knowledge that we've been called according to God's purpose and predestined to grow up like his Son (Rom. 8:28–29).

The way of control is the way of bondage. It is small, ingrown, and predictable. It is safe and manageable but it's always shrinking. Those who avoid FaultLines end up in a smaller world. They try to save their lives and end up losing them. But those who trust let go of their lives and end up finding them. Their world is ever expanding and more influential. The uncertainty of those who trust—which is what terrifies those who control—is the very thing that makes their lives bigger.

WHAT ARE THE FAULTLiNES?

Every one of us will find ourselves living on a FaultLine. Most of us already have—and maybe we're on one now—only we've been calling it something else, like a problem, and we've been trying to get away from it. This book is about embracing and leveraging that FaultLine. It's about "letting perseverance finish its work so that you may be mature and complete, not lacking anything" (James 1:4).

When I discovered that my "trials of many kinds," as James called them, were actually FaultLines designed to jar me back to the real normal, it completely changed my approach to spiritual growth. Looking back, I see that I was on one FaultLine or another for most of my life, and not because I was doing something wrong, but because God was trying to make me right. He was trying to do something beautiful with my abnormal life. FaultLines are the way he does it.

When I was growing up, my father would say, "If you don't pass this test, you'll have to take it again." He meant that God was trying to do something in whatever problem I was having, and if I kept resisting and running back to normal, the problem would recur again and again until I learned it. In this way, he said, most Christians don't really have thirty years of experience. They have one year of experience thirty times. They never grow, because they never change. And the older they get, the more resistant to change they become. "So learn it while you can," he used to say. When we learn it, we are growing—maybe four inches in six months—but the rest of the time we are not. FaultLines are seasons of growth.

There are as many FaultLines as there are people. And each one is different, according to the experience and the personality of those in them. But when we listened to the stories of our people, we noticed some common themes. These are the ones we've included in this book. Here's a quick survey.

A CALL

A call is a summons to partner with God in something he is doing, and it requires us to let go of something we are doing. We are drafted into a new life but tempted to bring as much with us as we can from the old life. Here we are chosen to do more with our lives than we imagined.

A CRISIS

A crisis is the sudden loss of something we have loved or trusted. It is ripped from our hands before we can let go of it, and we are tempted to become angry or defensive. But here we are called to put down stakes that will make us deeper and more convinced of our faith.

A CONFLICT

Conflict occurs when we are subject, over time, to things demeaning or unfair, and we are tempted to let those things define us. In our struggle to be free, we sometimes seek revenge in the form of "justice." But here we are called to a new identity and to something even better than justice.

A COMPROMISE

Compromise is a wilderness where the temptation to sin seems relentless. In our weakness, we are confronted with extraordinary opportunities. But here we are called to take back the wilderness of our lives.

A FAILURE

Failure is the dark prison of rejection, the feeling that we are inadequate, inferior, and alone. We are tempted to let this failure define us and minimize our imperfections. But we are called to confront them instead and to pursue a different kind of perfect.

A FORTUNE

Fortune is an unexpected and undeserved turn of events that improves our lot. We are tempted to own it or to trust it, but instead we are called to leverage it for something God is doing in this world.

A DEATH

Death is the ultimate separation from everything we have known, a movement from seen to unseen, from certainty to uncertainty, and the soul must decide where it is most at home. Like all mortals, we are tempted to leave our roots in this world, but we are called to grow more roots in another world.

In what follows, I hope to address the pressure, the risk, the hope, and the opportunity of each one of these FaultLines. Using characters of the Bible, I want to show that none of these FaultLines are unique to us. All of them have been endured by saints and heroes of the past. All were used by God to create something beautiful in their lives. I will show how we are tempted, as they were, to ask the wrong question in each one of these FaultLines, and then we'll explore what is, perhaps, the better question to ask.

Finally, we'll look at some of the things we can do to stay in each FaultLine until God has finished his work. I've called these sections "Talking Dutch," after my mother, who used to talk Dutch whenever she felt there was a lot at stake. It meant that she was going to be rather blunt and straightforward. She would not worry about hurting our feelings, and she wouldn't hold anything back. She would just say it. After that, we had a choice to make. When I was a child, I thought she was angry or just trying to get something off her chest. It wasn't until I had children of my own that I learned why Mom talked Dutch. She loved us. She was worried about us. But she was caught between her good sense and our free will. Not wanting to overpower us with her authority, and yet wanting to give us every opportunity to succeed, Mom would talk Dutch to make sure we knew not only where she stood, but how serious things were and how important it was for us to get them right. After Mom talked Dutch, there was no misunderstanding. So at the end of each chapter I want to "talk Dutch" to a few who are stuck in that FaultLine, because I think you still want to grow, but like me, you're probably averse to pain. Maybe you're at a critical point and you need someone to say things bluntly and with love, so you know how things work and how important it is for you to get them right. As you read, I hope you'll remember that I'm speaking as your brother, not your mom, and I am not an expert in these things. No one is. But I've had seasons where I've grown four inches in a few months. And I've had years where I didn't grow at all. I am speaking only from my experience, and sometimes I am speaking better than I know.

But this much is certain: I want to grow up. I always have. And while I am still inclined to avoid discomfort, I'm learning to see it as the normal aches and pains of growing. I like normal as much as anyone, but I don't want to get stuck at forty-two inches. I want there to be new entries on the board every few years until there's one that says "Christ is fully formed in you" (Gal. 4:19).

Isn't that what you want to be when you grow up?

2
A CALL
call waiting

On the eastern side of Southern California is an immense basin known as Death Valley. It's the lowest, hottest, driest area in North America. Less than two inches of rain falls there per year, and the temperature consistently reaches 110 degrees Fahrenheit. As a National Park, Death Valley covers five thousand square miles. But more than a desert, Death Valley also has towering mountains and shallow lakes, salt flats and canyons, rivers and meadows of wildflowers that bloom suddenly after a storm. It's a land of extremes—treacherous and gorgeous. It's the most godforsaken—and beautiful—country in North America. And the reason lies just below the surface.

Death Valley sits on a fault line. Many years ago, the earth shifted under the valley, gradually but violently, leaving huge fractures in the rock that have shaped the surface. The fault under Death Valley is called a *normal fault*, though there's nothing normal about it. The pressure in the earth's crust pulled the giant plates of rock apart, causing part of the earth's surface to sink (and form a basin) and another part to rise (and form a ridge of mountains).

The pressure pulling these giant plates apart is called *tension stress*. *Tension* is a Latin term that means "to separate" or "to pull in opposite directions." With billions of pounds of pressure, this tension stress pulls the earth's crust in opposite directions, causing the wreckage . . . and the grace and splendor known as Death Valley.

In a person's life, as in Death Valley, every FaultLine is a place of barrenness and beauty. It's disruptive, even violent, but it causes such elegant and breathtaking results that we are naturally drawn to people who have suffered and benefitted from a FaultLine.

All of us face circumstances that threaten to separate us from what is comfortable and familiar. They will pull us into a new life, and our tendency will be to try to salvage as much of the old life as we can. Herein lies the trouble.

THE TROUBLE WITH BEING CHOSEN

The most common tension we will experience is a call from God. Many of us will think we have not been called, but I want us to rethink that. A call is not simply a charge to be a missionary or a pastor. It's more secular than that; it involves everyone. A call is a defining moment—a knot in the timeline of our lives, when our options become clear and our decisions harden into destiny. The call is a predicament. It's both blessing and burden. It inspires us, yet costs us dearly. It is barrenness and beauty, violence and elegance, tension and grace. It is Death Valley. When called, some people come alive like wildflowers after a storm. They tower like a mountain over things that are mundane. But others shrink back and cling to the happiness they already know and eventually find it is too small to make them happy for long. A call is a FaultLine.

Last summer a middle-aged man told me of being called into ministry while he was still in college. "I was pursuing a degree in business," he said, "and I didn't want to settle for something like the ministry because of the crappy pay."

So he ignored the call as long as he could, "but it all came down to one night, when God told me to lay down my career in business." He was kneeling at an altar at the end of a service in the chapel.

"After a long struggle, I stood up and shouted, 'No, I won't do it!' I walked out of that church and finished my degree in business."

And how did that work out?

"Well, that was over twenty-five years ago," he said, "and I've moved twenty-three times since then. I never settled down. I couldn't."

So he went back to God with his business career in hand, asking for a do-over. Believe it or not, he got one. He enrolled in the classes necessary to make him into a minister, and today he serves a church in northern Michigan, where he's having the time of his life.

He said he makes three hundred dollars a week, "and that includes everything—with no health insurance." Now his oldest child wants to go to a Christian university, and he can't afford to send her. "But that's OK," he said. "We'll figure something out. No worries."

"So you were right about the crappy pay?" I asked.

"Yes," he laughed, "but I don't regret it. I've never been happier in my life!" And by his smile, I knew he meant it. He was living on a FaultLine—for twenty-five years!—and it nearly ruined him. But once he faced the right question and answered it, everything else changed. And what was that question? It is always the same: "Can God really be trusted with my happiness?"

WHAT DOES IT MEAN TO BE CALLED?

A call is a summons from God to get involved in something he is doing. Sometimes this means we do it professionally for the rest of our lives, like a minister or missionary, but more often it does not. We should not confuse full-time Christian service with the call, since service is only one expression of the call. At its core, the call is only a conversation God is having with us about something he is doing. So even though the call involves us, it is not really *about* us. It is always about the thing that God is doing.

One of the clearest examples is Moses. A middle-aged shepherd, he saw the burning bush and was so impressed that he volunteered immediately. "Here I am," he said, until he heard the rest. "I am sending you to Pharaoh to bring my people out of Egypt," said the Lord. But that was more than Moses could imagine himself doing, and so he argued, "Who am I that I should go to Pharaoh and bring the Israelites out of Egypt?" (Ex. 3:10–11).

Who am I? Ever felt that way? Moses' call was rooted in his weakness, not his strength, and the difference here is important.

When we're called on the basis of our strengths, we feel capable and prepared. We're optimistic about making a difference. We operate from within our experience. We use our degree. We can see ourselves doing this. Our call proceeds, in part, out of the affirmation that we have received in the past.

It seems a lot of people are called from their strengths. Like the boy David, they're not asking "Who am I?" They're asking, "Who is Goliath?" and they have all the confidence in the world that they can knock him down. They took a personality test or someone told them "You'd be great!" and so they signed up. Sitting in a room with a dozen young colleagues in ministry not long ago, I became aware of the difference between a call rooted in weakness and one rooted in strength. Like them, I had affirming parents who believed I could do anything. But I had problems with stuttering, shyness, and low self-esteem. My call to preach meant I would have to do the very thing that had made a fool of me for most of my adolescence. I would have to get up in front of people and . . . speak to them. I was not equipped for this. But somehow I managed. And while I am still shy and still stutter from time to time, I have never once stuttered while preaching. Whatever causes it—and I think it's rooted in my call— the stuttering goes away when I preach. Nevertheless, I know the feeling of terror, the fear of rejection, the thought of being a spectacle. Indeed, scarcely a week goes by when I do not feel ill-equipped for this job. My call is rooted in my weakness.

My younger colleagues seem to feel none of this. They are not plagued by the same doubt that has haunted me. They seem to know what they have to offer, and they're not wrong, but I noticed a chink in their armor—high levels of confidence often come with high expectations. And for all the good that high expectations bring, there is sometimes a terrible side effect. It became apparent when our conversation drifted to the subject of failure. Those called out of their strengths are more prone to be shaken by their failures. Whenever the task seems too hard, those called from their strengths can be easily disenchanted. "I don't need it, I don't deserve it," they said, one after another, "so I'll just move on." But for those, like Moses, who are called out of their weakness, *everything* seems hard or unfair. We are intimidated, but always from within, not from without. We often feel inadequate, but we are not easily overwhelmed.

A FaultLine occurs when we are called, like Moses, out of our weakness and not from our strengths. We go reluctantly, but we go, and as we go, we hear the voice say again and again, "Who am I?" We are no match for the thing God is calling us to do. How could we possibly be happy if we do it?

When we ask, "Who am I?" we assume that the power is in our hands. We take responsibility for the outcome and feel inadequate for the challenge. But in reality, the call is God's idea and so the outcome is always in God's hands. A call from God is never an offer for us to do something for God, but a forecast of something God will do through us. This means that when God calls us, we cannot say yes. We can only say no. God himself has already said yes. The call is a bold declaration of something God is going to do, and if we cooperate, he will do it with us. If we don't, he will do it with someone else. But whatever we're called to do, we will not have to make it happen. It is already happening. It has already started by the time we get the call. So when Moses asked, "Who am I?" God's answer was, in effect, "What do you mean, 'Who are you?' The question is 'Who am I?'" Which is exactly the question God answered: "*I* will be with you. . . . It is *I* who have sent you" (Ex. 3:12, emphasis added). It was never what Moses would do *for* God but what God would do *through* Moses.

In the end, Moses found himself bankrupt of all his excuses. He could only mutter, "Please send someone else" (4:13). So he went from "Here I am" to "Who am I?" to "Send somebody else." Sound familiar?

Many of us are like Moses. Our calling came in private. There was no one around to ratify it or to tell us how "perfect" we are for the job. So we suffer a chronic doubt. Each setback only confirms what we already suspect—that we are in over our head; or worse—that we are imposters who never should have tried in the first place. Like Moses, some of us suffer from low self-esteem. Some failure from the past still haunts us. We have some physical limitation. We have the heart of a lion . . . but it's the lion in *The Wizard of Oz*. We are reluctant, because we cannot let go of the familiar. We cannot part with whatever happiness we have to grasp the larger—indeed the only—happiness that can make us truly happy. Until we do, our souls will always wonder what might have been. And that is the cause of our misery.

So when we are called, we must not weigh the pros and cons. We must remember, as Oswald Chambers did, that "the call is God's idea, not our idea, and only on looking back over the path of obedience [do] we realize what is the idea of God."[1] But whether or not God comes through, "we have nothing to do with the afterward of our obedience."

Think hard about this and keep an open mind. Could God be calling you? Think of the call as occurring gradually with intensifying degrees of clarity and cost. The further you go into it, the clearer—and more costly—it becomes. As the call progresses, it passes through stages that require you to give consent. It's as if God raises the stakes each time and asks, "Are you still in? Will you go with me even here?"

This is the pattern in the New Testament. Take Peter, for instance. He was called to follow Christ more than once. The first time, he was fishing with his friends, and it meant only that Jesus should be his rabbi (Matt. 4:19). The second time, Jesus told him to deny himself and carry his cross (16:24). He used the same words—"follow me"—but the second time, they implied a cost that was far beyond making Jesus his rabbi. This time it meant Peter must be prepared to "lose his life" for Christ's sake (16:25). The next time, Peter was told that everyone would hate him if he followed Jesus (Luke 21:17), which raised the stakes even higher. And later still, Jesus told Peter to follow, meaning the manner in which he would die (John 21:22). The first and last call of Jesus is to follow him, but the meaning of it changes the further we go.

Now let's look at how our call progresses.

THREE STAGES TO THE CALL

In the early 1970s, Bell Telephone introduced a feature called "call waiting" that has become a standard in the telephone industry. Almost everyone has it in their plan. Call waiting allows us to take another call while we're in the middle of the first one. People who are introverts, like me, can't imagine why anyone would want a second conversation. Yet I am shocked by how many people do. Not long ago I was confronted by someone who wanted to know why I didn't take his call. I told him it was because I was taking another call and I already had a good conversation going. Why did I need another one? I think he left mad.

The second call can be as disruptive as the first one. Instead of the normal ring, you get a maddening "beep" reminding you that you still haven't answered that second call. You can ignore it if you want, but it won't go away unless the second caller gives up. And there is no gracious way to answer it and move on without the first caller feeling less important.

Recently, a columnist in *Good Housekeeping* received an inquiry from a person who clearly had been the first caller. "When I'm chatting with a friend," she said, "I feel hurt when she cuts me off to talk to someone else. . . . Shouldn't it be first come, first served?" I was incredulous, first that I was reading *Good Housekeeping*, and second that someone was actually upset at the prospect of not getting to talk on the phone.

The columnist replied, "It certainly should be," because even though there are exceptions, the code of ethics for phone calls dictates that "it's impolite to end a conversation to take another call." See what I mean?[2]

But sometimes the second call is so irresistible, so utterly important, that we take it anyway, and when we do, we hear news that is so compelling that we move on from the first call to the second. It's not that the first call doesn't matter. It's more that the second call is so urgent, so all-consuming, that we spend the rest of the day talking about it. That's how the call of God works.

We are minding our own business, neck deep in our own little world, when we get the call to follow Christ. At first, it only means that we make him our rabbi, our teacher. We become what Dallas Willard called apprentices or "someone who has decided to be with another person [Jesus], under appropriate conditions, in order to become capable of doing what that person does or to become what that person is."[3] But somewhere in the middle of that call, we get another call that is more demanding and more precise. We move through the outer circle into the middle circle. And then, right when we get comfortable in our new place, we receive yet another (third) call to go even further. This time it is more specific. More demanding. Yet we feel everything in the third call that we felt in the first—fear, uncertainty, inadequacy—and we face the same question too: "Can God be trusted with my happiness?"

Let's take a look at these three layers to the call.

THE CALL TO SALVATION

The first call is to salvation, the call to follow Jesus. The book of Isaiah has many such calls: "Come, all you who are thirsty; come to the waters . . . that you may live" (55:1, 3). We've heard language like this in sermons, but when we hear the call to salvation, we hear it as something more than just the words of a preacher. The words become personal. There is someone behind them. He is looking at us as if there is no one else in the room. The call is specific and uncompromising. And the action it requires is repentance (see Mark 1:15).

Repentance is not as quick or as easy as some make it sound. It's not an apology or admission of guilt. It's not a feeling, though it can be very emotional. It's not a promise to try harder, though we must certainly try something after we repent. Repentance is a change in the direction and course of our lives. By changing direction, we change our values. We have different priorities. We are no longer preoccupied with the same interests. And by changing our course, we change our way of life—the way we act, the way we treat people, the decisions we make, and so forth. In most cases, true repentance cannot be completed in one prayer or even in one night. It takes time to get into the place where you're ready to repent. And it takes time to work out the meaning of repentance in your life.

Recently, a man I'll call Rob was walking on the street in front of our church when suddenly he felt compelled to go in "just to see what was happening." A few minutes later, he was sitting in the morning service, wondering how the preacher knew so much about him. He said he thought someone had called the church and told us he was coming. Really! It took us awhile to convince him no one called. At the end of the sermon, Rob came to the front and just stood there. "I need to find God," he said, "because I've lost him." So Rob scheduled a meeting with one of our pastors, who led him in a prayer of repentance. In the last six weeks, the whole course of his life has changed. He has a long way to go, but already he's begun talking about his experience at work. He's recruited his entire family to come with him each Sunday. He's enlisted in small groups and says he is anxious to "do something for God" with the rest of his life.

That's the way a call to salvation works. Have you had one? Do you remember feeling like God was setting you up? It probably didn't happen all at once—it may have taken weeks, even months—but there was still that moment when you first realized this was headed somewhere. This was going to require a decision on your part. This meant that everything must change. For a lot of us, that's the most defining moment in our lives. How did God find me? Why did he come after me? It's that first call—the call to salvation—and we talk about it all the time . . . until we get the second.

THE CALL TO SIMPLICITY

The second call is to simplicity. *Simplicity* doesn't mean easy; it means a "singleness of purpose." The call to simplicity is a call to a single focus. Once we've received a call to salvation, the direction and the course of our lives change, but things get harder and more complex, not easier. We want to follow Christ, but we have to work. We have a family. We have friends and social obligations. Over time, we don't talk as much about our call to salvation—not because it's less important, but because other things come up. This happens to almost everyone, until they get a second call.

The disciples are an example of this. They were in their father's boat "casting a net into the lake, for they were fishermen" (Matt. 4:18).

"Come, follow me," Jesus said, which sounds a lot like the call to salvation, but in the next phrase, it becomes clear that Jesus meant something more: "I will send you out to fish for people" (4:19). Immediately, they left their nets and followed him.

The call of Jesus to these disciples was not simply a call to follow him, but a call to "fish for people." It was the call to simplify their lives around a single purpose. He was not asking them to change their occupation. In fact, they didn't. He was calling them to change their *preoccupation*. He was asking them to take on his mission and to make it the sole purpose of their lives. Too often we confuse Jesus' call to come and follow him with the call to be saved. We put the emphasis on the initial moment when the disciple chooses to accept Christ. But after the call to follow, there is always the call to enlist.

Sometimes this requires repentance, but more often, the action required is to reorient everything in our lives around a single focus, or if we can't, to let go of those things. Some people can do this and remain in their same career. Others must leave their career and pursue another one. The call to simplicity does not always change our occupation, but it always changes our preoccupation. Even when we keep our jobs, we do them for different reasons or, more accurately, for one reason. We "do everything in the name of the Lord Jesus" (Col. 3:17 NRSV).

Ross was the owner of a small business in our community. He grew up in the church and considered himself a Christian all of his life. He'd answered the first call to become Christ's disciple, but still he wondered if there was more to being a Christian than just going to church. Then he received another call—the call to simplicity. He said it was the combination of three things. The first was his decision to read through the Bible in one year, something he'd never done, and he still doesn't know what motivated him to do it. The second was that he started to hear things in the preacher's sermons he had never heard before. But the defining moment came when he took a mission trip to Zambia. At first, he noticed the abject poverty that everyone notices, but then he saw something else.

"These people were happy and so devout even though they had nothing," he said. "I wondered how they did it. They had more of God, yet they had less of everything else. Perhaps there was a correlation."

I remember the day he stood in the middle aisle after a service, waving his arms and saying, "There's a whole new economy, Steve.

There are things we value on earth that are not valuable in heaven, and there are things that are valuable in heaven that we do not value on earth."

So Ross implemented a new vision for his company. He established a new set of values, which he posted on the wall by the break room: "Serve others, not yourself! Be 100 percent reliable and on time. Treat others the way you want to be treated." He created three new positions for people who had just been released from prison. "It's a lot of work to keep them in line," he said, "but they need a chance." He started writing prayers to send to Christian leaders every Monday and set his computer to remind him every morning that it was time to pray for his staff. He gathered fifteen people into his home one night and raised seventy-five thousand dollars, then used the money to buy a well-drilling rig in Zambia, which has already provided clean water for fifty thousand people.

But Ross never left his business. One afternoon, while Ross and I were fishing in the Colorado River, I asked him why he never pursued a call to full-time ministry. He laughed and said, "Because I already have one." And he was right. Ross's call was not to change his occupation, but his preoccupation. He was using his business as a front to do what he really wanted to do, and that was to fish for people.

Have you heard a call to simplicity? If so, then you know firsthand how relentless and demanding it can be. But you also know that it has produced the most beautiful character in you. It has made you what you are. It's all you can talk about . . . so far! But brace yourself. You might have another call coming in.

THE CALL TO A MISSION

The inner circle is a call to a mission. When we are called to a mission, we are summoned to one particular cause and assigned a specific task. It may seem like an extension of our call to simplicity, but there are important differences. For starters, the call to a mission may require us to change our career. Even for pastors, it can mean that we do something else with the rest of our lives. It can mean a move to a difficult church or a foreign country. It can mean gaining more education, earning less money, working alone, or living in a place we're not fond of. It can mean putting our family on hold or living away from them for a season. A call to a mission is a call to a specific task that requires unprecedented sacrifice. It deprives us, at least for a while, of simple pleasures that other Christians seem to enjoy. It is a jealous and guarded friendship with God, under his anointing, while we accomplish a certain task, and then it is over. This is one of the telltale signs: There is a beginning and an end. People who have this call speak of being under orders or of carrying a mantle that others do not have to carry. They will not be in it forever. There will come a time when the mantle is lifted and placed onto someone else—usually someone younger—but for now they must do it. They must forego any privilege, postpone any dream, and risk their lives to join God in what he is doing.

Cheryl Beckett was a nursing student at Indiana Wesleyan University, who graduated in 2000 with a degree in biology. So promising was her career that Johns Hopkins University offered her a full scholarship for postgraduate work and the near guarantee of a flourishing career. But Cheryl felt God calling her into humanitarian work with the poorest people of Afghanistan. For six years, she served in hospitals and clinics that treated people with eye diseases, caring for those who were considered America's enemies at the time.

"I want to die to myself," she wrote in her journal. "What does that look like? How do I make that tangible?"[4] Cheryl was answering the call to a mission. On August 5, 2010, she was killed, along with nine others, when a band of terrorists attacked their vehicle while returning from serving in a clinic.

Cheryl denied herself many freedoms in order to abide by Afghan law and custom. Forced to live in an abandoned building, sometimes without heat in the Afghan winter, she suffered to fulfill her calling until, in the end, the mission that had cost her everything else, finally cost her life.

"Cheryl paid the ultimate price," said her father, Charles, to a crowded memorial service at her alma mater, "but in truth, she paid that price every day. She lived out God's Word. She adorned herself with his truth. . . . She shared Christ to those who were hurting and suffering. Make no mistake about it . . . there are a host of Afghan people today who know about Jesus because, like Nicodemus, in the cover of darkness they came and they asked, 'What are you doing here?' and she told them about Jesus."[5]

Sometimes we think of the call as a place to realize our dreams—and sometimes it is—but there are times when it can cost us our very lives.

TALKING DUTCH

Over the years, I've talked with hundreds of people who were interrupted at a certain time in their lives by a burning bush. They sensed that God was calling them into something more or something else. Some were called to bring their careers into the kingdom of God, and others were called to change careers. Some were called to serve the poor, teach in the university, or give large amounts of money away, and they just couldn't see how they were going to pull it off. So they wandered back away from the bush to the only happiness they had known, and ever since, they've been living on this FaultLine. If this describes you, then consider one of three possible responses; each is a form of trusting God in this FaultLine.

Perhaps you need to *choose*. As Moses "chose to be mistreated with the people of God rather than to enjoy the fleeting pleasures of sin" (Heb. 11:25), we can choose to follow God's voice, even if it leads us into the minority. We obey the call when we give our lives completely to Christ. We obey the call when we accept an invitation to do something for the kingdom of God, even though we don't feel qualified. We obey the call when we risk something or relinquish something that we have loved and trusted for years, because we believe that God is going to use it more fully without us. Choosing is a period of intense anxiety, but it usually comes down to a defining moment wherein we decide to drop our nets and follow.

Perhaps you need to *leave*. Many have chosen, but not all have left. Have you? To leave is a departure from what we once considered normal, what we knew or what was clear to us, for the purpose of risking a new kind of happiness. And when we leave, we don't look back. We venture into what is unknown. Our next step proceeds only from the assurance that God is with us in the present step. When we leave, we may be tempted to take as much with us as we can from our former life. We will volunteer. Help out around the church. Join something. Take some classes. Pledge a little money. Sign up for a short-term mission trip. And while this is all that God asks (for now) from some, there are those who are called to something more, and they use these things to negotiate an arrangement with God that allows them to hold on to their current lives. Maybe you were called, but you still haven't left. Maybe you haven't quite abandoned your current life because it would be too complicated for you. You are living on a FaultLine. Can God be trusted? Will he provide? Is the life into which you are being called really better than the one you'd leave behind? You'll never know until you go.

Perhaps you need to *persevere*. Like Moses, some of us have already chosen to obey God's call and have left. We did the hard thing. And we didn't look back. But that was awhile ago, and by now, things have slowed down a bit. The work is less inspiring and more complicated than ever before. Our souls are tired. We are tired of people who won't take chances or who won't forgive each other for the past. We are tired of living under pressure, of being judged all the time, of not feeling good enough for the work. We are tired of being caught between our work and our family or of accepting the blame when something wasn't our fault. We say we're done. We don't need this. We're not going to throw our family under the bus or waste our best years in this dead-end place. We can do something else, now watch us! So off we go. We try to find the call in another place. But sometimes the call is to the actual place we're trying to avoid. Sometimes the call is to Nineveh or Nazareth—anyway, somewhere not very glamorous, where we won't like it and we won't "succeed." Sometimes the call is to suffer for God's name (Acts 9:16). Just as the call reorients our vision of happiness, it reorients our vision of success. But at the core is the same old question: Can God be trusted with my happiness? Is the life I'm called into better than the one I'm leaving behind?"

When Jan was a teenager in Southern California, she spent many peaceful hours at the beach, reading, praying, and watching the sunset. One evening, she remembers, God spoke to her very clearly and said, "I want you to go to Africa."

"I didn't know why," she said, "but I knew I was supposed to go. Well, I didn't have any money, and I was too young, and that was so far to travel back then, so I put it off."

She graduated from high school and got married. Then came the children. Then the career. Then the grandchildren. Then retirement.

She was never idle. In fact, after retirement, she founded an organization called Tamar's Voice, which has helped many women who suffered abuse from the clergy.

Two years ago, Jan received an e-mail from a pastor who was hoping to start a ministry just like hers. Could he call her for advice? Better yet, would she come to his church for a conference?

"I was skeptical at first," she said. "But the more we talked, the more interested I became." What he was asking Jan to do was not extraordinary. It was well within her reach, except for one detail. He was from Kenya. And that's when Jan remembered her call almost sixty years ago. Now, at seventy-two years old, she would pursue it.

Last spring, Jan raised the money and flew to Africa to keep a promise made in her youth. She spent ten days there, and when she returned, she began raising more money to open a new center for abused women in Kenya.

If God has put a fire inside you—if he's asked you to join him in some cause—then leave what comfort you have for whatever he has called you to do. Don't argue. Don't negotiate. Don't think about how inadequate you are or about how little you have to offer. And don't think that it is too late. It's never too late.

Those who are happiest are those who have taken the greatest risks. They stepped out into a place that was uncharted and unsafe. They didn't know how it would end. They had nothing to do with the afterward of their obedience. They only knew what they were supposed to do *next*. So whatever God has told you to do, say yes. Venture into the unknown—where it is blessing and burden, tension and grace—for there in your Death Valley, you will find the most troubling and beautiful place on earth.

3

A CRISIS

the perfect storm

I t was the perfect storm," they said in Port Arthur, Texas, after a hurricane hit the coast in 1936, wreaking havoc and doing millions of dollars' worth of damage.

So far as we know, this was the first time the term was used to describe the weather. *The Port Arthur News* said it was the perfect storm because "seven factors were involved in the chain of circumstances that led to it."[1]

That's what a perfect storm is—the rare combination of atmospheric events that come together in perfect proportion and sequence to create a situation that is unprecedented and unmanageable. Google the term *perfect storm* and it will call up the 1991 Halloween Nor'easter that slammed into the eastern coast of North America from Canada to

Florida, with waves thirty feet high crashing the beaches. One buoy off the coast of Nova Scotia recorded a wave height of over one hundred feet. It inspired a book called *The Perfect Storm* (1997) and a movie by the same title (2000). These don't happen every year. They happen once or twice in a lifetime. Then you talk about them for the rest of your life.

I think the term is overused to describe our emotions or a really hectic day. When something goes wrong we might say, "Oh, it was the perfect storm." But perfect storms are more than setbacks or obstacles. They're a confluence of events so overwhelming, so relentless, so terrifying that one of two things will come of them: They will make us better, or they will make us worse. One thing is sure: We'll never be the same again.

Recently I watched a documentary of a sailor who raced against five others around the world. He didn't make it. He disappeared somewhere in the violent, extreme conditions of the Indian Ocean. One of the sailors who endured the voyage put it like this: "Imagine a twelve-story building coming toward you at fifteen miles an hour; then imagine somehow getting over it, only to be thrown down to the bottom and to look up and see . . . another twelve-story building only one hundred yards away; and another one after that; and then another after that."

I've been through a tornado, but I've never seen a storm like that.

And yet, I have.

"Pastor, I need you," he says over the phone. "Can you come to my house?" Ron had just had the eleventh surgery on his back, each more radical than the last and each without success. With every surgery, there was the usual recovery with medicines and high deductibles. He'd been disabled since I knew him.

When I got there, he showed me a dozen letters he'd found in the bottom of his wife's dresser drawer.

"I don't know how I found them," he said. "I guess I was just snooping around."

He began to read them aloud, and as he read, I became sick to my stomach. They described in vivid detail the rendezvous, the sex, the deep feelings his wife and her lover had shared for more than a year. They were planning to leave their marriages as soon as they got up the nerve so they could be together.

We set up a time to talk to her together, and when we did, she abandoned the marriage and ran off with her lover. Within a couple of years, one of their children was unmarried and pregnant. It was another blow to this man who had served the church as a youth sponsor, a trustee, and a short-term missionary. Ron had built the altar for our new church, and now we were gathering around it to pray for God to sustain him while everything was coming loose.

Eight months later, the baby was born with a birth defect to her heart. The doctors said she would not survive.

"Pastor, can you come and baptize my granddaughter?"

"Of course I can."

So I drove nearly two hours to the hospital and prayed with the family. Then I got a little dish from the nurses' station and filled it with water. I blessed the water and anointed that baby only minutes before she passed away. I cried with the parents and then stepped into the hall to collect myself.

"Pastor, can I see you for a moment?" Ron asked, coming right behind me. He pulled himself close, within a foot from me, and whispered, "I've heard the father of that baby is going to leave my little girl as soon as this ordeal is over. What am I going to tell her?"

And all I could see was one twelve-story building after another crashing into this guy. *That* is the perfect storm. And while most of us don't live in conditions quite that extreme, it's all relative, isn't it? The only difference between Ron's story and ours is the size of the waves, and when you're in the middle of them, they're all big.

Over the years, I've seen many perfect storms. Even now I can replay the mental images and feel the tension. The doctor bursts into the waiting room before the surgery is supposed to be over and tells us our friend is full of cancer. "There is nothing I can do," she says, "It won't be long. This will go very quickly." One by one, we cover our mouths. Soon even the doctor is crying.

A midlevel manager with twenty-one years in the company is called in and released. "It's nothing personal," they tell her. "We just can't afford you anymore." And that's the end of it. She has thirty days. Where will she go? "I don't know," she says. "I'm too old to start over somewhere else." And it seems she's right. She's applied dozens of times since, and each time is another wave of rejection.

In my care of souls, I have seen all of these crises, like storms, sweep across members and families in my church. The news is always sudden, always devastating. Even when you can explain it, it doesn't make sense. Even when you see it coming, you are never prepared. If you talk to people who've been through one, some will tell you that it happened in a moment and others will tell you it happened over time. But all of them will tell of the day, or the moment, when all hell broke loose. They know where they were. They still remember the feeling.

A perfect storm is a kind of FaultLine. It's a crisis that comes—either gradually or all at once—and forever changes the landscape of our lives. It's a sudden jolt that knocks us off our feet and sends us scrambling for answers, for help, for something solid to stand on. Like storms, everyone has seen a crisis or been in one of their own, and everyone is afraid of them. There is no stopping them. They are the result of forces far above and beyond our control. You can't fight them or outsmart them. You can't even run from them. You can only hunker down and wait them out. No doubt, you've seen a few in your lifetime. Take a moment, right now, and recall one or two of them. Maybe it was a friend who lost a lot of money when the market crashed. Maybe it was someone who was diagnosed with a rare disease. Or someone whose home was destroyed by a flood. Or someone whose child was injured, beaten up, or arrested for drunk driving. Think of a time when someone you know was suddenly overwhelmed by a crisis. Write their names in the margin of this page.

Then think, not of getting them out of it, but of keeping them in it.

ANATOMY OF A PERFECT STORM

Like a FaultLine, the perfect storm occurs when forces beyond our control converge in the right sequence to cause chaos that threatens to destroy us—a once-in-a-lifetime nightmare. It could happen twice, but once is enough. It's not the result of something we've done wrong. It's not punishment. It's dumb luck. It's unfair. And hard.

The crises I've seen in more than thirty years of experience are complex. They're a confluence of six forces, each beyond our control, that play off each other. And these forces are each made worse when combined with the others. Let's look at them briefly.

First is our *expectation*—the general optimism we have for life overall. Most of us believe life is elastic and, though it may be stretched for a while, will always return to normal. There are ups and downs, but in the end, everything will be alright. This optimism isn't blind. Even people who have had a lot of setbacks, people who have nothing, often find a pattern of small pleasures that have become for them a kind of normal. And they will protect this "normal" as fiercely as anyone else. The most despairing people in the world are those who have no expectations and no normal.

A second force in the perfect storm is our *faith*. In faith we believe that God is good and that he wants to protect the normal. We believe that the Bible promises this. In faith we pray, and in faith we hope for miracles. In faith we declare things "done." We oversimplify. Faith makes it easy to believe in a miracle when, really, more work is required. But the trouble is not with our faith in miracles, but with our finite understanding of "good." From where we stand, we cannot see all that is good or how the crisis could bring good about. Trapped in this world, we consistently want for ourselves less than what God wants for us. We want things that are not necessarily wrong but could never make us happy. And when we lose these things, we think faith is the way to get them back. If we are honest with ourselves, we know that, in a crisis, our faith is often the belief that we will get back what we once considered normal. The power of a crisis is that it loosens our grip on these things and prepares us to receive something more.

A third element is the *loss*. This is the moment we feel threatened. It's the thing that was not supposed to happen. It devastates us. Quite often this is the element that we refer to when we say, "All hell broke loose." In a crisis something is always lost—something we value, something we need—and this loss occurs at different levels. On the surface, we lose something tangible, like a friend, a job, a privilege, or something we've depended on for a long time. But on another level, we lose something intangible. Sometimes we don't even notice it at first, but over time, it hurts worse and lasts longer than the first loss. The man who discovered the letters in his wife's dresser drawer lost more than his wife. He lost his self-esteem. While a counselor tried to heal their marriage—and could not—my friend spent many nights alone (his first loss) where he contemplated what it meant to be unwanted (his second loss). The same was true of the woman who suddenly lost her job. In addition to the loss of income was the insult of being unnecessary to the company she had served for twenty-one years and the inability to find another job quickly. Look over the names you wrote in the margin above. No doubt, you can tell immediately what their first loss was. It was their income, their job, or their health. But what else did they lose? Almost every loss is connected to other losses, and usually the hardest ones are internal.

This leads to another element of the storm: *futility*. This is the helplessness we feel when our efforts don't work. Crucial to a perfect storm is the sense that we are losing control. Sometimes control is taken from us all at once, as in one swift disaster, but more often it is taken from us piece by piece. Four years ago, my sister's husband was taken to the hospital after a fluke accident. The next day, he had surgery, and did not wake up as soon as expected afterward.

That was no problem, we were told, because he would come out of it soon. Only he didn't. Then they told us not to worry, because there were several other options available. One by one, we watched those options go away, until finally, they moved him to another facility where, they said, he might still make a full recovery. He lived another week, and then he was gone. It was the perfect storm. On top of our profound loss, against all faith and expectations, was the growing sense of futility. We were losing control, piece by piece. We had been dealt a handful of options and then felt as if somebody took them away one by one until nothing was left in our hands. We were completely vulnerable. Sometimes when this happens, we blame, because to blame is to find a reason where there is none. We try to explain what can never be fully explained. It's as if we cannot bear the thought of being vulnerable with nothing—not even an explanation—to protect us from random things. If we were honest with ourselves, we would know that the hardest thing to deal with is not the loss itself, but the feeling that we are not in control. Sometimes we get angry, and sometimes we blame, but both are a form of control. And once it's apparent that neither will work, it leads to . . .

The next element of the storm, which is *fate*. Fate occurs when the future collides with the present. When it becomes apparent that things are going to be this way from now on, this is our fate. This is the new normal. And it's very different from what we imagined. Sometimes this element occurs suddenly, as in the case of a natural disaster, but usually it does not. When combined with the other elements, fate can be a devastating blow. Whenever something goes wrong, our expectations and our faith—the "normal" and the "good"—convince us that somehow everything will be alright. The more tenaciously we hold to our "normal" and "good," the harder it is to reconcile with the future that is fast becoming clear. Finally, there is a moment—even in a crisis that mounts gradually—when it first occurs to us that things will not end the way we had hoped. This is often the time when we quit, because if we cannot control how things will end, then at least we'll control *when* they will end. They will end when we say so. Look again at the names in your margin. This is the day they still talk about. This is the video still playing in their minds. Their crisis was not simply their loss, but the future that they feel stuck with. And the further this is from their vision of the normal and the good, the harder was the storm that hit them.

There is one more element to the perfect storm that I call, for want of a better word, the *collateral damage*. This is all the other things that get adjusted by the crisis, but were not part of the crisis in the first place. These are the details that not only complicate the crisis, but make it worse. They compound the harm. In divorce, it's the children or the mutual friends. When we lose our job, it's the hassle of relocating, the trouble of making new friends in another city, or even the fear of losing the next job too. When we're diagnosed with a rare disease, it's the expense and the side effects of the treatment, or the plans that will have to be put on hold.

A crisis is never a moment, no matter how sudden and devastating it is. It's the perfect storm of things that lead up to the crisis and then come out of it. It's the convergence of many things, and each one of them is intensified by the others. Any one of them, alone, is not enough to throw us into a crisis. But together, they can be devastating. They can leave behind an internal restlessness born of fear and confusion that makes us wary of the future.

AN EXAMPLE OF A PERFECT STORM

Picture this. Paul is a seventy-year-old paraplegic who, only months ago, was walking. He underwent a surgery to clean out his carotid arteries, and a surgical malfunction caused a massive stroke that left him paralyzed, confined to a wheelchair, and barely able to speak. It's a heavy loss for this lovely couple, now in their sunset years. But Paul and his wife Ruby are Christians. Paul has been a minister all his life, and Ruby thinks it's time to collect on all the work that he's done for the Lord. So she calls in a favor from God. One afternoon, when Ruby's expectations are at their peak, she calls her pastor and asks him to come to their house to pray. Ruby has faith. She has decided that God is going to heal her husband and that this is the day he will do it. When the pastor arrives he finds them in the living room, ready to "do this" as if "this" were another kind of surgery, only easier and faster. When the couple is ready, the pastor reads the appropriate Scriptures and then anoints Paul with the oil of healing. The pastor leads the couple in a prayer and then . . . there is an awkward silence.

Nothing happens.

"Paul, did you hear the pastor? Get up!"

Then a pause.

"I can't," he says.

"Yes, you can. Have faith! You have to believe that you've been healed."

Paul stares into the eyes of his wife, willing himself to move, but, still, there is nothing. He looks away and his eyes fill with tears.

"I'm sorry," he says.

"Why don't you try again? Here, let me help you."

The pastor watches helplessly as Ruby tries to help her husband up, but her efforts are futile.

In those few seconds, the future has been shoved violently into the present. This will be the new normal. This is their fate. As reality seeps in, the two hold each other and begin to weep. Once they've collected themselves, they look to their pastor and say, "What have we done wrong?"

The minister who told me the story still can't figure it out. Neither can I. Time after time he's seen God do miraculous things to save him in a crisis. But this time was different. The prayer that saved *him* could do nothing for Paul and Ruby.

Look over the story once more, and you'll notice that all five elements are present in Paul and Ruby's perfect storm. This is a full-fledged crisis. This is a FaultLine. From here, things will get either better or worse. After this, or rather in it, this beautiful couple will get a new vision of God that makes him either closer to the world or further from it. The crisis will require them to see themselves as either more precious to God than they imagined or more insignificant to this world than they feared. They will either believe God is with them, or they will wonder if he is against them. The mystic John of the Cross called it a "dark night of the soul," when the soul feels "that God has abandoned it and, in His abhorrence of it, has flung it into darkness . . . [or] that God has forsaken it."[2] It can't go both ways and it can't stay the same. It's a FaultLine.

When this couple goes to work on their image of God, they will touch one of the most fragile strands of their life. Changing their view of God this quickly, this radically, is the spiritual equivalent to having surgery on one's spinal cord. They will come out better, or they will come out worse. From this crisis will emerge a new pattern to their lives. Over time, they will learn (because they must learn in order to survive) new ways of thinking about the future, new ways to temper their expectations, new ways to talk about their faith, new ways to treat each other. They will be either wiser and softer and more human, or they will be angry, calloused, indifferent, and more removed from humanity. They will either be humble and quieter, or they will be dogmatic and loud. They will either be more aware of the eternal, or they will hold tenaciously to what little of their lives is left. They will either move gradually toward things unseen, holding loosely to what little they possess in this world, or they will become paranoid and possessive of each little thing that time will strip from their hands anyway.

In that split second, Paul and Ruby were forced to let go of their "miracle" and to face the deep and abiding fears that confront everyone in a crisis.

Invariably, the question we ask in a quiet crisis is, "Why?" Why did God allow this to happen? Why doesn't he answer prayer? Why can't things go back to normal? First we get angry. Then we suffer. Then we quit. People on the FaultLine of a crisis instinctively wonder why, because to understand is a form of regaining some control. If we can make sense of it, then maybe it won't overwhelm us. Or maybe we can back up and work on something that contributed to our crisis, and the crisis will go away. Things will get back to normal.

The trouble with the question, though, is that the answers never satisfy us. Even when the answers are "right," we are still left with the storm's consequences. So we ask again, this time in ways for which there are no answers, as if we are trying to stump the crisis. The question why? is sometimes the vengeance we take on a crisis when we think that it follows the same rules of logic we do. Only it doesn't. So people who keep asking why get stuck. They never change anything because they are always only trying to understand. In spite of this, "Why?" is always the first question we ask.

But it better not be the last.

SHIPWRECKED

There is a better question to ask in the FaultLine of a crisis, and this one will take us further toward the core. This is where we decide whether our lives will get better or worse. It's the question that occurred during a real storm in the apostle Paul's life.

Buried in back of Acts (ch. 27) is one of the great stories of an ancient maritime shipwreck. While most shipwrecks do not occur because of a storm, this one did. And Luke's account of it is like something you'd see in a movie. Picture the scene.

Paul was onboard a ship headed for Rome. He was a prisoner and one of 276 passengers on an Egyptian vessel that was 140 feet long and 36 feet wide with a 33-foot draft. It was a big and sturdy boat, but it had a couple of flaws. First, it didn't have a rudder but employed large oars on both sides of the boat to steer it. Second, it had only one sail. When the tailwinds were strong, it would move really fast, but it could not sail into the wind, making it vulnerable in a storm. At the beginning of this scene, a severe storm was brewing in the northeast that would change everything. Some scholars have placed the voyage in the middle of October, the height of storm season. In just a few weeks, the seas would be closed for the winter, so the captain decided to go for it. The destination was Phoenix, only forty miles away on the southwest side of the island of Crete. With an average speed of about four knots, they could make it in less than a day.

Once they put out to sea, "a gentle south wind began to blow" (Acts 27:13), and they thought it would be a smooth sail to Phoenix. But then a strong wind from the northeast swept down the island, and the ship was caught in its path. Interestingly enough, the Greek word used for this northeaster wind is *typhonikos*. It was a typhoon, blowing somewhere between 70 and 170 miles per hour, and because the ship had only one sail, it couldn't sail into this wind. It could only sit there and take its beating. Within minutes, the whole thing was out of control. The crew started passing ropes under the bow of the ship, attempting to hold it together. Then, fearing that the ship would run aground on sandbars and be torn apart, they lowered the ship's anchor and let the wind drive it along. They trusted this strategy the entire night. In the morning, the wind had not subsided, so they started throwing cargo overboard. This made the ship lighter, but it didn't lessen the pounding of the storm, and so on the third day, when the storm had not relented, they threw the ship's tackle overboard. Then they were left with nothing but each other and the ship.

That's when everyone hit bottom: "When neither sun nor stars appeared for many days and the storm continued raging, we finally gave up all hope of being saved" (Acts 27:20). Ever been there?

Replay the video in your mind, and you'll notice several of the elements we referred to in the perfect storm. At the beginning there were expectations: "When a gentle south wind began to blow, they saw their opportunity" (v. 13). Then there was the loss of the ship: "The ship was caught by the storm and could not head into the wind . . . [so the men] passed ropes under the ship itself to hold it together" (vv. 15, 17). This was followed by the futility of trying to turn things around: "They began to throw the cargo overboard. On the third day, they threw the ship's tackle overboard with their own hands" (vv. 18–19). Finally, there was the creeping awareness that this was their fate; this was the way it would end: "We finally gave up all hope of being saved" (v. 20).

Every day, the pattern is repeated in someone's life. Maybe yours. Maybe you had great expectations, and then something interrupted your "gentle south wind." It was a typhoon that came rushing out of nowhere and blew you off course. First, you tried holding it together, but nothing worked. The storm was relentless. Even after taking almost everything, it kept pounding you for days. Maybe you've let a bunch of stuff go—friends, church, jobs, family—and still the storm rages, and so you've surrendered any hope of being saved. Maybe you're a storm-wearied skeptic who thinks that things will never get better. Maybe you can't afford to hope anymore. You can get stuck there for years, you know. Maybe you're a weathered, sea-weary cynic who thinks that nothing will change because, well, nothing has. Maybe you feel you can't afford to hope any longer.

THE DEEPER QUESTION

Back on the ship, in the worst of the crisis, Paul spoke up. And in his words, we hear the soul asking a different question. When Paul

71

spoke, he gave us a glimpse of the first signs that he would not only survive this FaultLine but actually grow because of it. Something solid, something beautiful, was coming out of the crisis.

"I urge you to keep up your courage," he said (v. 22). And then he said that an angel had appeared to him the previous night and told him, "Do not be afraid. . . . God has graciously given you the lives of all who sail with you" (v. 24). In the middle of the crisis, Paul went back to something he was told the night before. It's as if there were two realities side by side. One was something he could see (indeed, something everyone could see); the other was something he was told. One reality was seen and the other unseen. In the one, they had lost their tackle and were losing their ship. But in the other, God had already granted safety to everyone aboard. Both were true, and they were true at the same time. And the harder the one hit, the more Paul clung to the other.

"Keep up your courage," he said, "for I have faith in God that it will happen just as he told me" (v. 25). This is real faith. It's the capacity to stand firm in the storm, because you know how to hear God's voice. You believe in another reality. You see the presence of God where others panic. In *SoulShift*, we talk about faith as the shift from Seen to Unseen or the shift from Ask to Listen.

> Faith's work is not to ignore the stark reality of our enemies lying in wait surrounding us. Rather, faith's work is to remind us of another reality even greater than that of the enemy. Faith sees that our enemies have indeed surrounded us. But it also sees that our God has surrounded our enemies, that "those who are with us are more than those who are with them" [2 Kings 6:16].

Faith does not speak things into existence. It simply sees what is already in existence, though still unseen to those who live by sight alone. Faith sees a world that runs alongside this world, and it lives according to what we see in both worlds. Faith sees through the eyes of the soul. It sees now what everyone else will acknowledge later. Only faith sees it now.[3]

Storms are great places for SoulShifts to happen. They are times when everything underneath is moving. Things we love or trust are suddenly taken away. The once-steady ground under our faith begins to move until life itself is trembling and swaying. And the question the soul asks, while everything else is giving way, is, "What do I truly believe?" Do I really believe what I was told? Do I truly believe in the authority of things I have heard but do not yet see? Do I believe in the other reality? Because if I do, then once the storm passes—and it always will—I will emerge with a heightened awareness of the unseen. I will have a better capacity to hear the voice of God. But first, you have to believe—to really believe—what you were told in the Scriptures.

People who live on a coast, like people who live over fault lines, are required by law to build their homes differently. They have to construct their buildings to withstand the winds or the sudden shifting of the earth's crust, so they can endure the crisis without toppling over. They have to make their buildings crisis-ready. And the secret lies deep in the foundations. In traditional settings, most of the weight of the building rests on the walls and is equally distributed from the bottom to the top. But when builders construct something to withstand a storm or an earthquake, they drive pylons deep into the earth and attach most of the building's weight to these pylons. Yet there is some flexibility built into the pylons, so that when the earth begins to move, the building will sway without toppling over.

This idea of anchoring something deep and tying everything to it—while allowing for some movement and play—is a good way to think about the role of our beliefs in the time of crisis. Sometimes our beliefs become unnecessarily rigid and fixed. They depend upon things turning out exactly as we've planned. So when the storm hits, our beliefs topple instead of sway because there is no flexibility built into them. Perhaps you're in the middle of a storm right now. If so, it's worth asking yourself, "Have I begun to believe in something that God did not really promise me? Do I have good people around me—who know the Scriptures and who love me—and are they capable of telling me the truth?"

FAULTLINE READY

We need pylons, driven deep into the earth, that are firm but flexible, that tie everything together, and that will keep us from toppling over. And where are we to find them? Right here, in our story of Paul's perfect storm. Here are a few pylons to drive deep into our souls during a crisis.

We will lose something, but we will not lose everything. In the perfect storm, Paul told the sailors to "keep up your courage, because not one of you will be lost; only the ship will be destroyed" (Acts 27:22). Every storm takes something away from our "normal." We must cut it loose and throw it overboard, like the ship's cargo. It was never God's plan to protect our expectations. Things may never be the same again, but then, maybe that isn't such a bad thing. We'll have to adjust. Learn new patterns. Make new friends. Live within our boundaries and under new limitations. But with God's help, we can do this—even if we don't want to—because we must.

God may not rescue us, but he will always cover us. Paul said, "I have faith in God that it will happen just as he told me. Nevertheless, we must run aground on some island" (Acts 27:25–26). Whether the storm will subside, only God knows. But no matter what happens, he will be with us, even when we feel most alone. The three Hebrew children (in the Old Testament book of Daniel) who were thrown into the fiery furnace knew that God could deliver them, but they didn't pin their whole religion on his answer. They said, "The God we serve is able to deliver us from [the fire] and he will deliver us from Your Majesty's hand. But even if he does not, we want you to know, Your Majesty, that we will not serve your gods or worship the image of gold you have set up" (Dan. 3:17–18). God didn't rescue them from the fire. Instead, he went into the fire with them. When the king saw it, he jumped to his feet and screamed, "Look, I see four men walking around in the fire, unbound and unharmed, and the fourth looks like a son of the gods" (v. 25). Some believe this "fourth" man was none other than some form of God himself. We must not connect the goodness of God with our safety or with the idea of getting out of the storm. Too often we ask for things God never intended to give us in the first place—not because they are wrong, but because they are so much less than what he intends for us. He comes to us—in the storm—and bids us to walk on the water. This is so much more than we ever imagined for ourselves and so we settle for asking him to simply calm the storm. We ask him to make it easier, when he wants to make us strong. We must remember that God alone knows what is good and that he is in charge and will do whatever he pleases. This may not always match our idea of "normal," but if God is in it, then the storm is the safest place to be, which leads to another pylon to anchor our faith.

Unless we stay in the storm, we cannot be saved. Even after the sailors had unloaded the ship, things were still coming apart. And so a handful of soldiers began lowering the ship's lifeboat. Who could blame them? They'd had fourteen days of this, with no food and little water. The boards under them were coming apart. The deck was floating under water. It was every man for himself. Then Paul said, "Unless these men stay with the ship, [we] cannot be saved" (Acts 27:31). It's an odd thing to say in a storm, isn't it? "Unless we stay in it, we cannot be saved." This defies every instinct. But we must believe that what God is doing in us, or for us, is not in spite of the storm, but precisely because of it. There are things he is trying to give us that we hesitate to accept, because we cannot accept the way that he wraps them in a storm. And he does it not because he is trying to break us down, but because there is no other way to give these things to us. By their very nature, they require a storm to transmit them. So if we stay in it, we can be saved. If we defect, we will not. And this leads to a fourth pylon.

When the storm is over, we'll believe fewer things, but we'll believe them more. When the ship finally ran aground and the surf kept pounding the stern to pieces, some people grabbed a plank or a piece of the ship and floated safely to shore (Acts 27:44). The whole scene strikes me as a metaphor for the way storms cause us to unload our convictions and biases, throwing them overboard like cargo, and cling to whatever is left of our beliefs. And whatever is left will get us safely to shore. Just recently I talked with a woman about a crisis that happened in her life a year ago. She said that even though she wouldn't wish that crisis on anyone, neither would she give it back now that she's grown so much through it. "I've gotten rid of a lot of biases," she said, "because they were just unfounded. Now I believe less than I've ever believed, only I believe it more."

TALKING DUTCH

Perhaps you or someone you love is in a storm. Maybe you're asking, "Why did God allow this?" but your soul is asking something else. Can you stay in the storm and believe what you were told? Who has the line on reality? Who can say what will happen? Perhaps you should find a community—maybe a small group in your local church—where you can be totally honest. Perhaps you should tell them, "I'm in the middle of a storm," and let them remind you of these truths that you can sink into your soul. Perhaps you should tell them of things God did not say and you have believed them anyway. Maybe you could benefit from hearing how God has steadied others by using these same truths. Would you be willing to do this with a handful of your closest friends? The best ones will not try to fix you. They won't fill up the room with advice, like Job's friends did. They'll simply listen and pray. What you need in this perfect storm are friends who can believe for you. You need friends to lower you through the roof, so to speak, and put you right in front of Jesus so he can heal you. You need to be reminded of a few unshakeable things you already know but have let go of when you started fearing for your life. You need to say them again, out loud, to yourself and to others.

My friend, to believe in things that have not yet happened, to speak of things that are not as though they were, requires a faith that goes deep into our inner core. It is informed, but optimistic. Firm, but flexible. It absorbs the blows. It steadies us. And when the storm finally passes—it always does!—it leaves a depth and a richness that cannot be had except by those who have weathered the perfect storm.

4

A CONFLICT

a cause better than justice

Homeless Andrew" was the street name of a man who lived on the streets of New York City. He became the focus of public attention when he was featured on the "Walk Over" segment of the *Opie and Anthony* radio show. Andrew offered them cake he was saving in a box.

> ANTHONY: "What's in the box?"
>
> ANDREW: "It's a cake. . . . Treat yourselves."
>
> [He holds it up so his guests can see it.]
>
> OPIE (laughing): "What is it?"
>
> ANTHONY (laughing): "It's something cinnamon. . . . It looks good, but I'm not touching it. You eat it. No, put it down for a second."

[Homeless Andrew places the box on the ground and Opie stomps on it with both feet. More laughter.]

ANDREW: "Ohh, come on man. That's not nice . . . that's not nice! You know I earned that . . . come on, man. . . . I earned that."

[More laughter.]

[Opie taunts homeless Andrew, waving a $100 bill and throwing it at his feet. More laughter.]

[Homeless Andrew sits quiet. He is speechless while the mocking continues.]

OPIE: "Ahh, he was so happy to show everyone his cake. It was so cringing and yet fun to watch. Oh, that is going to be a great download, man. He was so proud of his cake. That was the holy grail for homeless people. Ahh, the poor bum."[1]

The day after Opie posted the video, the duo was shocked to learn that not everyone was laughing. In fact, most were not. When the video went viral, the public weighed in: "This makes me sad. . . . That homeless guy was twice the human as those two animals who teased him." Others were not so kind: "We're out of options here; time to pool our money and hire a hit man!" Someone else wrote, "I wish I believed in hell."

A few months later and because of the public's outrage, the two hosts decided to pay Andrew another visit.

OPIE: Hi Andrew . . . we missed you . . . we missed you so much.

ANDREW: Thank you.

ANTHONY (laughing): Hey, I love your Bob Denver haircut.

ANDREW: You know, it's what the Lord has given me.

OPIE: You're right. You gotta work with what the Lord has given you. You're the Bangladesh Bob Denver. The Bangladesh Gilligan.

[More laughter.]

ANTHONY (laughing): Bob Denver . . . and Gilligan . . . that is really good, man!

ANDREW: I cannot be choosey about what the Lord has made me.

OPIE: Well, is there anything else that comes to your mind about the last time we spoke?

[Andrew can't remember.]

OPIE: I think I threw a $100 bill at you. Do you remember now?

ANDREW: Oh yeah. You guys are helpful to me. Thank you. You know I have to go through hell out here every day.

OPIE: Well, Andrew, because of the cake thing, we've decided to bring you something. We felt a little bad about the cake thing and we got a bunch of Danishes and cupcakes for you . . . oh, and some bagels.

[More laughter.]

ANDREW: Oh my . . . thank you. . . . God bless you. Happy Thanksgiving to you guys.

OPIE: Happy Thanksgiving to you, Andrew.[2]

What do you feel when you read stories like this? What do you want to do, or what do you wish would happen to people like them?

Opie and Anthony have been fired many times, once for starting a rumor that the mayor of Boston was killed while transporting a female Haitian prostitute (1998), then again for coaxing a couple to have simulated sex in the vestibule of St. Patrick's Cathedral during a holy day (2003), and again for allowing a homeless man to say, over the air, what he'd like to do with Condoleezza Rice (2007). These two bullies once even teased a homeless man, whose leg was literally rotting with infection, telling him that he needed to wear a different baseball cap if he hoped to get any money in New York. Their "gift" to him that day was a Yankees ball cap so he could beg with decency.

Do you know anyone like Opie and Anthony? They can be arrogant, self-absorbed, mean, and manipulative predators who take advantage of other people's niceness. They can posture themselves as friendly, funny, intelligent, or generous, but in reality they are condescending. They use rudeness as a kind of power over others. They victimize people with their humor. They oppress their subordinates with their high standards. They mock us, yet we follow them. Sometimes we venerate them. They are deplorable winners, and God knows they need to be put in their place. But God also knows that he had better do it himself or it will ruin us.

People like this are a kind of FaultLine, though I suppose the more proper term would be "conflict."

LIVING ON THE FAULTₗₗNE OF CONFLICT

The word *conflict* comes from a Latin term (*conflictus*) that means "to strike together, or to press and squeeze." It describes the rub of two people or agendas that are crossways with each other. It's the abrasiveness of working for someone who is demeaning and unfair. It's the wound of being disregarded or tyrannized by someone who is self-absorbed, who abuses power, or who is just incompetent, but whose position makes it hard to ignore them. There's a very good chance that you know a few people like this. There's a chance that you've suffered one or even that you are suffering one now.

Sometimes it's their fault and sometimes it's ours, but there are seasons in our lives when we are subject to conflict. We are put into a place—either under someone or in between forces—where it is hard to live a peaceful and quiet life. We don't know what we did wrong, but we are suddenly on the outside, suddenly labeled, and the more we try to avoid it, the worse it gets.

If you find yourself on this FaultLine, your trouble has likely come from one of only three things: incompetence, injustice, or insensitivity.

If you are subject to *incompetence*, then you have to deal with someone who is erratic, paranoid, self-serving, or doesn't know what they're doing. Maybe you need their permission or their recommendation. Maybe you're responsible to them. Take David, for example. After he was anointed to be king, he still served the incumbent king Saul and was forced to deal with Saul's schizophrenia. One moment Saul was asking for David to play his harp, and the next moment he was asking for David to be killed. He was an erratic, paranoid, and unfit king, but he was still in charge, and so David was required to submit to him.

If you are subject to *injustice*, then you are suffering at the hands of some tyrant, even though you have done nothing wrong. Maybe it's for political reasons. Maybe it's a misunderstanding. Or maybe it's just for sport. But someone has it in for you, and you cannot avoid them. Think of Joseph. The governor's wife propositioned him day after day, but "he refused to go to bed with her or even be with her" (Gen. 39:10). So one day she accused him of raping her. When her husband heard this, he retaliated by throwing Joseph into prison. There was no investigation or trial. To our knowledge, Joseph was never even asked his side of the story. He was swiftly eliminated, and the governor's wife was never confronted. Joseph stands for all who have done what is right and got in trouble for it. They are victims of someone's politics or pandering. They're the collateral damage of a business that cheats, a spouse who deceives, an organization that downsizes to fatten the salaries of a few at the top, or a judge who turns a blind eye to the evidence because he's trying his own case.

If you are subject to *insensitivity*, then you are probably in charge of something but not in control. You are under people who are slow, stubborn, critical, and demanding. You are doing the best you can, but it just doesn't register with them. When sociologist Randy Hodson researched the most common complaints among workers today, he found three things that consistently undermined the dignity of people at work: (1) abuse of power, (2) overwork, and (3) unrealistic expectations. Workers said that their employers "under-hire or hire incompetent people. . . . They make us file reports and don't read them. . . . They don't affirm us, or even notice what we're doing. . . . They let equipment run down and take too long to fix it. . . . They waste money and complain that they can't pay us. . . . They make snap judgments that affect us but they don't keep us informed. . . . They pressure us to work overtime," and so forth.[3] Sound familiar? Moses dealt with people who were insensitive. For forty years he was the proverbial Boy Scout who led the old lady across the street. From the moment Moses was "hired," the people refused to follow him. They threatened to ignore him, then to replace and ultimately kill him. Moses lived on the FaultLine of conflict.

All three of these—incompetence, injustice, and insensitivity— are sophisticated ways of stomping on someone's cake. All three are seasons that we cannot avoid. The randomness, the violence, the relentless abuse of these people is so overwhelming that it can ruin us.

Or it can strengthen us. Conflict is a FaultLine that will blow two thousand feet off of our lives, or it will create a beauty and an innocence that is attractive to the world, even to the jerks. It all depends on how we answer the question of the soul.

HELL HATH NO FURY

One of the most famous conflicts in the Bible involved two women vying for control over one man's loyalty. Each considered herself a member of his family. Each believed she was part of God's plan. The story is complex and twisted, but at the bottom lies a question I believe the soul asks during conflict.

Abram was seventy-five years old when God promised he would become the father of a great nation. Ten years later, after nothing measurable had happened, God reappeared to confirm it.

"Look up at the sky and count the stars," he said. "So shall your offspring be" (Gen. 15:5). But the next chapter opens with the haunting reminder that "Sarai, Abram's wife, had borne him no children" (16:1). This is the second time God appeared to Abram. Each time,

God made the same promise, disappeared, and then nothing happened. It is much easier to wait for something backward—knowing what we know, to say that Abram should have simply trusted God. But it is harder to wait for something forward—before you know how it will end—and that is what Abram and Sarai were called to do.

Sarai had an idea. Since God had promised many children, if she was unable to have them, then she would get creative. And in those days, there was only one way to do it. "The Lord has kept me from having children," she said to Abram, "so go into my Egyptian servant and perhaps I can be built through her" (16:2, translated from the Hebrew). The servant was Hagar, an Egyptian slave girl who was given to Abram by the pharaoh of Egypt (see Gen. 12:10–20). Hagar was the property of Abram's family, and Sarai "gave her to her husband to be his wife" (16:3).

At Sarai's bidding, Abram "slept with Hagar and she conceived" (16:4). That's when the trouble began.

As soon as Hagar conceived, her status changed. She was still the slave girl of Sarai, but now she was Abram's other wife. Immediately she began to despise Sarai. The word *despise* means to curse, to be critical and demeaning, and to hold in contempt, but it is hard to know exactly what it meant. Robert Alter translates it, "Her mistress became slight in her eyes,"[4] which is probably closer, since the ethics of the day allowed for Sarai to get rid of Hagar if she suspected any competition for Abram's loyalty. It's more likely that Hagar's contempt for Sarai as a non-child-producing wife was internal, that she kept it to herself, but Sarai perceived it anyway, and that's why Sarai "mistreated Hagar" (16:6)—meaning she was harsh, demanding, overbearing, and even quick-tempered.

Have you heard the saying "Hell hath no fury like a woman scorned"? The story of Sarai and Hagar has twice the fury. Oddly enough, both women found themselves on the FaultLine of conflict. Sarai felt contempt from her rival, who was using her pregnancy as a kind of power. And Hagar felt the scorn of her mistress, whose plan had just backfired. Each vied for Abram's loyalty. Sarai insisted that she was the first lady of the house, but Hagar reminded her that she was the mother, the one favored by God, and now Abram's wife. The conflict continued for weeks, with Sarai envying Hagar and Hagar despising Sarai.

The writer of Proverbs said there were four things under which the earth trembled and the last two were "a contemptible woman who gets married, and a servant who displaces her mistress" (Prov. 30:23). One can only imagine how hard this situation must have been for Abram. It was time for him to "man up" and establish some order in the house. But Abram did not. When Sarai asked him to get control of the situation, he refused and said, "Your slave is in your hands" (Gen. 16:6).

What was that supposed to mean? Wasn't that "slave" really Abram's wife? Didn't he have an obligation to her?

It was clear to Hagar that she would receive neither justice from her mistress nor protection from her husband. She would always be Sarai's property and the surrogate to Sarai's legacy, not her own. Once she knew this, she ran away.

IN DEFENSE OF HAGAR

Sadly, Hagar's been used as a scapegoat by a lot of writers, including some in the Bible. Isaiah called her "the other woman." Paul said she was "that slave girl" who reminded him of the law, and given some other things Paul said about the law he didn't mean that as a compliment. John Calvin said she represents those who have defective faith. Oswald Chambers said she represents "things that keep us back from God's best."[5] She is roundly criticized by people today as the home wrecker who interfered with Sarai's family. But all of this criticism ignores the plain fact that this kind of arrangement was not only legal in that day, but also common. It was not forbidden—even in the Bible—until much later. It was permitted and regulated by every major religion in Hagar's day. To put it bluntly, Hagar had done almost nothing wrong. It wasn't her fault that she was born Egyptian. Or that she was handed over against her will to Abram as a bribe to get him out of Egypt (see Gen. 12:14–16). Or that God made a promise to Abram that he hadn't kept yet (Gen. 16:1). It wasn't her fault that she conceived easily and Sarai didn't, or that Sarai used her to build her own legacy. It wasn't her fault that Sarai distanced herself from the child she manipulated Hagar to conceive. Indeed, the child was never called Sarai's child, but always Hagar's child. And, given her low status, it is unlikely that Hagar had anything to do with this. It is more likely that Sarai decided to disown the child and that Hagar, being the biological mother, could not disown him, even though she knew he was already unwelcome in Abram's home. And it was not Hagar's fault that Abram—her husband now—would not defend her. Hagar had lived in the family for ten years, ever since the pharaoh handed her over as property to Abram, and there had never been any trouble. But suddenly she found herself caught between forces she could not control. As Christians, we may want to side with Abram and Sarai. But even though we venerate them, this was an embarrassing moment. Abram and Sarai were the perpetrators of most of Hagar's trouble.

Hagar stands for everyone who has lived on this FaultLine, who has endured the scorn or mismanagement of someone in authority or who has been subject to people who are demeaning and unfair. She stands for those who work for incompetent bosses, who are maligned or marginalized because of their faith. She stands for those who have been silenced or disregarded by the powers that be or who have been threatened and fear for their lives. She stands for those who have come to Christ and discovered that their spouse or friends are not supportive. They have been ridiculed and minimized. Hagar stands for people who are trapped inside systems that are inflexible and demanding, that belittle them and deprive them of their dignity. I know physicians, teachers, politicians, and several pastors who feel trapped between the will of the people and the expectations of those in control. What they have in common is the feeling that they have no power. They are vulnerable. They are victimized by people who are demanding or by systems that are unfair. And the only way they know to survive is to do what Hagar did—either despise the powers that be or run from them.

DESPISING OUR ENEMIES

When we despise the powers that be, we undermine them. We talk about them behind their backs. We calculate ways to make them pay politically. We imagine conversations with them in our head, and we get the last word. One woman who was cheated out of a single day's vacation told me, "I got what was mine in the end, because I took enough supplies from the cabinet to keep busy for years to come." One man feels that he is undercompensated for his work and so he "borrows" his employer's tools and never brings them back as a way to get what is rightfully his. Someone else sits in the lounge and mocks the manager, the principal, or the dean, hoping to erode the trust of others. A college student goes into great detail while asking for the class to pray for her parents, because she wants them to know how mean her parents are and how heroic she must be for staying with them. These are all ways of getting our pound of flesh from Sarai because she has made life difficult for us.

AVOIDING OUR ENEMIES

When we run from the powers that be, we avoid them. We withdraw. We withhold our support. We do our own thing. We quit trying. We hide inside the organization and no longer worry about improving it. We only want to keep our jobs, to get tenure, or to get our inheritance or whatever else we are owed, but we no longer participate in the family or in the organization. One teacher tells me that she is only putting in her time, because she's tired of fighting the system, tired of the incessant flow of undisciplined kids and over-protective parents, and tired of deteriorating schools. Once she despised them, but when the leaders of the school did not come to her defense, she ran. Now she is only protecting herself against more hurt and disappointment.

Despising and running are two ways of getting revenge. One is active and the other passive, but both seek to gain some of the power Hagar thinks she has lost. It's an attempt to insulate herself from the abuse and to stand up for her rights. And who can blame her? After all, revenge is the most common response to this FaultLine. It's the refusal to sit down and take whatever is handed to us. To run from those who oppress us, or, if we cannot, to secretly despise them is the revenge we take on people and systems that put us on this FaultLine.

THE QUESTION OF THE SOUL IN CONFLICT

So Hagar ran. And God found her near a spring in the desert on the road to Shur. It was the road that went straight into Egypt. Hagar was running home. But home was three hundred miles away, and most of it went through the wilderness where there was nothing to sustain her. She had decided it was better to die than to remain a victim of Abram's mismanagement and Sarai's abuse. It was here where the angel found her and called her by name: "Hagar, slave of Sarai, where have you come from, and where are you going?" (Gen. 16:8).

The answer was that she had come from Canaan (16:3) and was going back to Egypt (16:7). But since the name Hagar was not Egyptian but Semitic—in other words, since it was likely given to her by

Abram after she left Egypt—she was going in the wrong direction. The question put to Hagar concerned her identity and her destiny: Did she know who she was and where she was going? And it is apparent that she did not. She had forgotten who she was and had no idea where she was going, and so her reply—"I'm running away from my mistress"—didn't answer either question. Hagar didn't know who she was because no one up to now had even called her by name. This was the first time anyone had used her name. Not Sarai, not even her husband, had called her by name. Isn't that strange? She had always been the property or "that slave girl" of Sarai. She had been the surrogate mother, the "other woman," the one who caused all the trouble. But to the Lord, she was "Hagar," the only woman in the story, indeed the only woman in all of early Hebrew literature to whom God spoke directly. She was thus favored by God. She was "seen" by him. She was as much an object of his favor as she was of Sarai's wrath. But Hagar had forgotten this. And I think we forget it too.

This is the question our souls ask in the FaultLine of conflict: "Who am I, and where am I going?" People who suffer under tyrants and fools forget who they are and where they are going. Because they forget who they are, they believe they are what their critics have called them. And because they forget where they're going, they are always running away. They are doing what they think they have to do to avoid the conflict.

On the FaultLine of conflict, it is essential to remember our identity and destiny. If we forget who we are, then we will act like someone else. And if we forget where we're going, we will keep running away.

REMEMBERING OUR IDENTITY

When our kids were small we drilled this into them: "You belong to God and to us. We love you, and you are precious in our sight." Then they'd go play with their friends, and occasionally, over supper, we'd hear that someone had called them a name. To counter this, we taught them the difference between a fact and an opinion. We'd say, "There are facts and opinions, and you must always be careful to keep them separate. Most things fit into one of these two categories, and if you confuse them, you might believe things that aren't true. Or worse, you might *not* believe things that are true." Then we'd play a game. I'd make some statements and ask them to tell me if they were fact or opinion. I'd say, "Mommy's hair is black"; "Our house is next to the church"; or "We live in Michigan." And they would shout, "Fact, fact . . . that's a fact!" Then I'd say, "Mommy's hair is beautiful"; "Our house is not as nice as their house"; or "Michigan is the best place to live." And they would say, "Opinion, opinion . . . that's an opinion." We'd play this game everywhere—in the car, at the table, on a walk, or before they went to bed. Why? Because so much is riding on a child's ability to distinguish between fact and opinion. After awhile, the game started to get boring. After all, there are only so many ways to disguise an opinion as a fact. So we quit playing it. Then one day, when our son was in fifth grade, he came home in a fluster. Someone at school had laughed at his new shoes and said they were ugly. "You must be poor," they said, "because you wear cheap and ugly shoes." It really bothered him. He couldn't get it out of his mind. So I resurrected the game.

"What they said about your shoes . . . was that a fact or an opinion?" I asked.

"An opinion," he said, but he didn't laugh. We could see that the comment really hurt him. We all went quietly to bed that night because something in our home was changing. Our son went to bed wondering if his shoes were really ugly. Our daughter went to bed wondering what would happen if they laughed at her shoes. And we went to bed wondering whose opinion mattered most to our children.

As we get older, we tend to draw our identity increasingly from things outside of ourselves. We tend to think that we are whatever the public says we are. Even people who appear overconfident, who "don't care what anyone thinks," fight this same tendency. It is as though there's a voice from within and a voice from without. The one from within is God's own voice, and it says, "You are my beloved in whom I am well pleased." The one from without is a voice that says, "You are nobody, and you will always be nobody until you can prove that you're somebody." The problem for those on the FaultLine of conflict is that they can never prove to their oppressors that they are somebody. It doesn't matter what Homeless Andrew says to the two jerks holding microphones. He cannot impress them. They won't let him. He can't even change their minds. The only power Homeless Andrew has is the power to assign to someone else the right to name him. He cannot stop Opie and Anthony from calling him "Bangladesh Bob Denver," but he can stop himself from thinking it matters. He can assign the right to identify him over to God and strip Opie and Anthony—even if only in his mind—of any power over him.

The same was true for Hagar. She couldn't stop Sarai from mistreating her, but she could deprive Sarai of any ability to determine her identity. She could choose to listen to the voice from within, to the one who found her by the road, and she could know that she was not "the other woman" or the collateral damage of Sarai's harebrained scheme. She was Hagar. She was seen. She was favored by God.

This mind-set is essential when we suffer opposition: What is in us is more important than what is in them. We are not only acted upon, we are acting. We cannot make someone like us, respect us, or agree with us because we cannot control what others do. But we can control what we do in return. And what we do in return will affect both them and us. The other person may have started it, but if we can collect ourselves soon enough to remember who we really are, then we can deprive them of any sovereignty over the outcome, because whatever happens from here depends on them *and* us, not just on them. In this way, "the lips of the wise protect them" (Prov. 14:3). In this way, a gentle answer turns away wrath (Prov. 15:1). In this way, a good defense gives an answer for the hope that lies within us (1 Pet. 3:15).

My friend, if you are on the FaultLine of conflict—if you suffer the tyranny of incompetence, injustice, or insensitivity—it is essential that you return to that voice within you, the one that found you by the road, and that you anchor your identity there. It is essential that you truly believe what you say you believe, that you let the Word of God define you from within and not some lesser voice from without. If you are a child of God, you are not what your critics say you are. You are not even what you are trying to be to spite them. You are God's beloved, nothing more and nothing less, and the sooner you remember that, the more good this FaultLine will accomplish.

REMEMBERING OUR DESTINY

When the angel appeared to Hagar, he reminded her of her identity and spoke into her destiny: "I will increase your descendants so much that they will be too numerous to count" (Gen. 16:10). It was more than Hagar could have dreamed for herself. But she was about to forfeit it all if she ran away. God had favored her. She had "seen the One who sees me" (16:13), but she had to stay in the FaultLine to qualify. By running away from Sarai, she was running away from God's favor. By choosing to die in the wilderness, she was choosing to forfeit all the Lord would do for her.

So the angel told her, "Go back to your mistress and submit to her" (16:9). That must have seemed impossible. She was told, in effect, "Go back to your FaultLine and submit. Go back to your boss. Go back to being a servant. Go back to your responsibilities without insisting on your rights." These words must have been as hard for Hagar as they are for us. In fact, I can't think of many things that come harder for Christians today, especially for those who serve under harsh rulers, than the habit of submission. The more educated we are, the more powerful we are, indeed the older we are the harder it is to submit. We think that by submitting we somehow endorse the rude and incompetent acts of those who rule over us. We think it dehumanizes us and makes us second-class citizens. But this is not what is meant when God calls us to submit. To submit is not simply to take our beating. No . . . it's much harder than that.

To submit is to invest in the good of the person over us. To submit is to pray, support, obey, and protect the interests of the leader who is in charge. To submit is to defend them when they're not around.

It is to help them accomplish their goals. It is to realize that even though they're giving us a lot of grief, they probably have grief of their own, even as Sarai did. To submit is to empathize with them over their misery, over their barrenness, over the way they have maybe "cursed" themselves. To submit is to respect them, even if we cannot like them, and to follow their orders to the best of our ability. To submit is the habit of holiness. So often the real source of our conflict is not the injustice of those who are in charge, but our own unwillingness to submit. It is not always the antics of our enemies, but our own unholiness that causes us so much grief.

When fire fighters try to contain a forest fire, they will sometimes go ahead of the fire, into places where the fire has not yet reached, and burn it down before the fire gets there, because they know that fires burn on resistance. It is the nature of fire to consume things that are still standing, to burn only those places that have not already surrendered to the fire. By burning the ground in front of the fire, the fire fighters eliminate the resistance, so when the fire reaches the ground they've surrendered, it burns itself out.

If you live on the FaultLine of conflict, you are tempted to resist your enemies because you are trying to make room for yourself. But if you submit—that is, if you eliminate your resistance—the conflict will burn itself out and you will have left room for God.

"But it isn't fair," some will protest. "Don't we have a right to justice?" No doubt Hagar felt this way, but she soon learned that God's favor was more valuable than justice. If she had God's favor, she could endure any injustice because God's favor would trump it. I am embarrassed over how long it has taken me to learn this. For too long I have wanted only justice. I wanted things to be "fair." I wanted the Opies and Anthonys to pay for their crimes. I was paying too much attention to Sarai and not enough attention to God. I forfeited the favor I needed by trying to give Hagar the justice she deserved. In the end, "justice" is only the name we give our revenge when we can't stay on the FaultLine any longer. Watchman Nee wrote,

Nothing has done greater damage to the Christian testimony than our trying to be right and demanding right of others. We become preoccupied with what is right and what is not right. We ask ourselves, "Have we been treated justly or unjustly?" and we use this to vindicate our actions. But justice is not our standard. . . . You ask me, "Is it right for someone to strike me on my cheek?" I reply, "Of course not, but do you want only to be right? Is justice the only principle of your conduct?" Right and wrong is the principle of Gentiles and tax-gatherers. Our lives are to be governed by the cross and [by] the perfection of the Father.[6]

This does not mean that we simply allow perpetrators to have their way. We have every right—indeed, we are obligated—to protect ourselves from people and things that would defile us or compromise our integrity. We do not always have to give in. We may protest, or object, or even prosecute if we must, but never for the sake of vengeance. Never for the sake of "giving them what they deserve."

Here, in the FaultLine of conflict, we must discover where our real power lies. It does not lie in our version of justice, whatever that is. It lies in God's freedom to favor us. It does not lie in what we can do to our oppressors but in how we possess ourselves in spite of our oppressors. Our power lies in the mastery we have over our own souls. When we discover our power there, God uses this FaultLine to establish our identity in him. It is there—under the scorn of injustice or inside the raw and dirty politics of the day—where God finds us, where he sees us, where he utters our name.

TALKING DUTCH

If you find yourself pummeled by forces you cannot control and subject to their opposition or incompetence, no doubt, everything in you cries for justice. But forget about justice for a moment and think about yourself first. If you are on the FaultLine of conflict, then you are standing at the border between the past and the future. You cannot stay here for long. You must make a decision. Behind you are those who have done you wrong, those you feel cannot be trusted. Perhaps you fear, mock, despise, or ignore them because of what they have done to you. You can either go backward or forward, but you cannot stay where you are.

To go backward is to even the score, to make sure those people pay. It is to let them know who's boss and to make them regret doing what they did to you. It is to get to the bottom of it or try to change their minds. It is to convince them that they were wrong or, if you cannot, to get your pound of flesh.

I love justice, and so my first instinct is always to go back. I want to teach them a lesson, to let them know they can't get away with this. I want to make them play fair. I want to get what I have coming to me, and, of course, I want them to get what they have coming too. But do you realize how many wars are perpetuated by this very desire to go back? Can you imagine how many divorce settlements, land disputes, family feuds, or church splits have happened because someone went back in the name of justice to settle it? If you go backward, you will probably get some form of justice. You will help them to see that they were wrong or at least that you are as good as they are.

But to go forward is to let go, to forget what they owe you, to risk that they may not learn anything and instead may take advantage of you. To go forward is to establish boundaries that keep others from stealing your future, and keep you from dwelling on the past. To go forward is to relinquish your power, the power of being hurt, of being owed an explanation. It is to choose your own behavior, not according to what was done to you or to the premise that you *must* feel a certain way, but according to the way that is in you. To go forward is to be free. It is to choose your own actions today as if it were a brand-new day.

Jesus told us to go forward: "Love your enemies. . . . Bless those who curse you and pray for those who mistreat you" (Luke 6:27–28). This might feel risky to us, but it is only because we want to go backward. If forgiveness and reconciliation feel like we are giving our enemies a pass, it is only because we are still dwelling on the past. We still remember the score and feel like they owe us.

But when we go forward, the possibilities change—for us *and* our enemies. Doors are opened. New channels are cut into the most stubborn of hearts. This doesn't guarantee that our enemies will change, but we can be sure of this: They will never change if we keep trying to go back. We must go forward.

Recently while I visited the home of a young couple in our church, a fight broke out between their two children who were playing upstairs. I wasn't privy to the fight, but from what I could tell, there was a scuffle for power over something that both of them wanted. The youngest child came down screaming for justice. He was mad—really mad—and he wanted his daddy to go upstairs and settle it. But all the father did while the child poured out his heart was to coddle him and whisper, "I know . . . I know . . . you're going to be alright now; I've got you . . . I know . . . I know."

To my surprise he did nothing—absolutely nothing—to settle the score with the other child who was still upstairs. He just held the one who came to him, and then he did something more. He started to whisper the child's name. Again and again, he used the child's name and said, "I know . . . I know . . . I've got you now; you're going to be alright."

At first, it made no difference. The boy only wanted justice, and to be totally honest, I wanted it too. Then something remarkable happened before my eyes. The longer the child listened to his father's voice the more he believed him. And the more he believed him the calmer he got. Soon, the young boy quieted because he knew he had his daddy's attention. Very slowly, the favor he got from his father became more important than the justice he owed the child upstairs. And do you know what else? The bond between them—father and son—was stronger now, precisely because of the scuffle.

Who is the person or where is the place that is holding you down? I can't promise that you will one day get out of it. But I can promise that if you stay in it long enough, God will see you, and there he will whisper your name.

5

A COMPROMISE

lead us into temptation

Since their beginning almost seventy years ago, game shows have become popular in every part of the world. Millions of people watch them. They've produced their own stars—like Guy Fieri and Vanna White—and even their own liturgy like, "Is that your final answer?"

One of the most popular game shows in recent years was called *Deal or No Deal*. The contestant chooses one of twenty-six numbered briefcases, each containing a different sum of money from one dollar to one million dollars. The contestant then tries to determine the amount of money in his or her briefcase through a process of elimination, by selecting and opening the remaining briefcases one by one.

Meanwhile, watching from upstairs behind smoked glass is a shadowy figure known as the "banker." As the game proceeds, the banker calls in offers, tempting the contestant to trade his or her briefcase for a guaranteed amount of money. They have only a few seconds to decide. Deal or no deal? If the contestant says, "Deal," they walk away with the money the banker offered, no matter the amount of money in the briefcase. If the contestant says, "No deal," the contestant walks away from the guaranteed money and continues to open the remaining briefcases. As the contents of more briefcases are revealed, the banker's offer either increases or decreases. In other words, the contestant is not really playing alone but against the banker.

You can play the game online, just for fun, so I did. I had the banker over a barrel. Finally he offered me thirty-seven thousand dollars, so I sold him my briefcase and walked away a happy man . . . that is, until they opened my briefcase and revealed that it was worth three hundred thousand. Then I was mad! I got skunked more than two hundred fifty thousand dollars. I never should have sold that briefcase, and I wouldn't have if I'd known how much it was worth.

Deal or No Deal is built around that kind of suspense. The question for the contestant is whether the banker's offer is higher or lower than the amount in the chosen briefcase. Are they negotiating up or down? Each contestant begins with a dream of winning easy money. She thinks she has a pretty good chance. She'll look at twenty-six briefcases, pick one, and when she's made her money, walk away. No contest. But what she has forgotten is that she is competing against the establishment. The banker is trying to get the best of her. Patient and wise, the banker knows how to motivate her to give up the briefcase and minimize her winnings. The establishment has rigged the game so that it provides the maximum amount of drama while the giving the contestant the minimum amount of money.

I cannot think of a better analogy for temptation.

Temptation is like an advertisement to get something for nothing. We might think of temptation as a struggle with our desires, and sometimes that's all it is. But just as often, it involves two super-powers doing battle over turf in our souls. When we are tempted, often we are not playing ourselves but the establishment. We are playing against dark and sinister forces that have calculated our chances at winning and stacked the odds against us. We are drawn by innate desires to get something easy, and we usually overestimate our chances of winning. Our adversary is patient and wise like the banker in *Deal or No Deal*. He knows how to motivate us to risk what we already have for the slim chance of getting a little bit more.

WHY ARE WE TEMPTED?

You might think God would do everything in his power to keep us out of that kind of contest. But in fact, he does not. Sometimes it seems like he leads us into it. We pray, "Lead us not into temptation," but then we read how "Jesus, full of the Holy Spirit . . . was led by the Spirit in the wilderness where . . . he was tempted by the devil" (Luke 4:1–2). Why does the Spirit do this? To be sure, "God cannot be tempted by evil and he himself tempts no one" (James 1:13 NRSV). But why does he lead us into places where he knows we will be tempted? It seems like the last thing we would expect from some-one who is full of the Spirit is to be tempted by the Devil. And even if he was in a place of temptation, we cannot imagine he would have gone there on purpose. It must have been an accident. Why would someone who was filled with the Spirit go into a place where he could lose it all?

"Led by the Spirit . . . where he was tempted by the devil." These words create tension, not only because of the contradiction, but because we find ourselves living in a similar tension. We are led by the Spirit, and yet we are still vulnerable to temptation. Some translators try to calm the tension by making it sound coincidental. One says, "Jesus was led by the Spirit . . . [and] he was tested by the devil," as though both events were happening at the same time but were not connected. But this translation doesn't resolve the larger question of why, in the first place, the Spirit led Jesus into a situation where God knew he would be tempted. And it doesn't resolve the tension we find ourselves in when we are tempted.

Jesus went through every one of our circumstances to model what true humanity can do in each situation when infused with the Holy Spirit. When we see Jesus in his true humanity, we see not only the Son of God, but also the Son of Man. He is the perfect revelation of both God and humanity. When we see him, we see who God is and also who we may become in our humanity. Hebrews says, "Because he himself suffered when he was tempted, he is able to help [us] who are being tempted" (2:18). It is important, then, that "we . . . have a high priest . . . who has been tempted in every way, just as we are—yet he did not sin" (4:15). The story of Jesus—especially his temptations—is our story as well. When we watch him in the wilderness, we are watching ourselves. When we see him overcome his temptations, and even leverage them, we are seeing what we are capable of when we are full of the Holy Spirit.

It is not always wrong for us to be tempted. True, sometimes our temptation arises from our own evil desires—John Chrysostom is known for saying that we create a scene where there isn't one—and this is the kind James talks about (James 1:13–15). But at other times, like Jesus, we are not even looking for trouble but suddenly find ourselves in a situation from which we can't escape. We are confronted with an opportunity to do what we know is wrong, and we find ourselves in a struggle.

HOW ARE WE TEMPTED?

The temptation to do evil often plays off something good. Temptation is not evil in itself. It simply raises the possibility that evil will result. Because temptation plays off something good, we can never be rid of temptation. Like the banker, it will always be there making new offers: "Deal or no deal?"

Those who study the human brain tell us that thousands of stimuli whirl around us all the time. Each one is a potential distraction, and we cannot control most of them. Our brains are always noticing external and internal distractions (called "ambient neural activity"), if only subliminally. Even when we are thinking about one thing, our brains are always making other connections. Always reconfiguring or filing. Always inviting data in and forcing data out.

For instance, I am sitting on my living room sofa at 5:30 in the morning. All is quiet. There is nothing to think about except this chapter. Or is there? The ticking clock and the distant rumble of a motorcycle remind me it's later than I think and maybe I should go to work. A book on the theology of work catches my eye, and I think I should finish it. Out of the corner of my eye I can see a half cup of coffee, now cold, and a two-day-old donut. Smelling the old coffee makes me want to make another cup. In the back of my mind are last night's conversations, which trigger an avalanche of details about my daughter's upcoming wedding. I notice that I haven't moved in so long that my foot is asleep.

Most of these stimuli occur at the subconscious level while I focus on this chapter, and all of it occurs simultaneously within seconds. As they occur, my brain is subconsciously sorting, filtering, and keeping me on task. With practice, I can get better at staying on task, but I cannot completely eliminate distractions. There will always be impulses. Tendencies. Habits. And many of them will be triggered involuntarily.

David Rock likens it to sitting in a crowded theater and watching a play, then having members from the audience randomly jump onto the stage and shout something or do something crazy for about two seconds before leaving the stage.[1] We can't avoid our distractions or our temptations, because we can't control the audience. We can't make everyone stay in their seats.

On top of this is the virtue or the good that God has already put in our hearts, and some of our temptations play off existing virtue. "If you are the Son of God . . ." the Tempter says (Matt. 4:3, 6). Well, he is! There is no *if* about it. The impulse to turn stones into bread would have had no traction if Jesus was not actually able to do it. The Devil hasn't tempted me like this, because I know I can't turn stones into bread. He might have tempted me to stop at a restaurant.

"I will give you all [the world's] authority and splendor . . . if you worship me," the Devil continued (Luke 4:6–7). This would not have been tempting if Jesus did not already desire the world. If the invitation to worship the Devil seems ludicrous to you, as it does to me, it's not because we're too spiritual to be fooled. It's because we don't desire the world as Jesus does. We never had it, as he did, and so we don't want it back. As Savior of the world, his desire for the world is only good, but it was also the fertile ground the Tempter used to try to dissuade him.

The same is true with us. The power of the impulse for anger, for example, is often tied to a love for justice. What makes us precise, what makes us strive for excellence, often makes it more likely that we'll be critical or ungrateful. You love to help people, so if you're not careful, you will try to control people. You love righteousness and integrity, but you might be cold or unmerciful to someone who is failing. Find your greatest virtue, and you will likely find your biggest vice somewhere nearby.

That strength or virtue, placed in us by the Holy Spirit, is like the briefcase at the contestant's side. Will he sell it or keep it? Does he really know how much it's worth? Temptation becomes a contest between two superpowers—the One who gave us our virtue and the "banker" who wants to buy it for cheap—and we are caught in the middle. Like the banker, our adversary knows full well what our strength or virtue is worth. He knows what is in our briefcase, and so he lures us with things that are worth less. Deal or no deal?

We cannot control the offers he will make. We cannot even control all the impulses or tendencies he will use to hook us. But we can control whether we make the deal or not. We may not always have free will—because sometimes our options are limited—but we will always have free "won't." We have veto power.[2] We can choose whether to act—to deal or not to deal—with any offer the Tempter places before us. When he drops thoughts into our heads, he may play off things we have seen before, and we cannot control the impulse to be interested in them. But we can control whether to dwell on them. Whenever we are tempted, there is always a brief, even if undetected, moment in-between the involuntary desire for something and the voluntary movement to act on it. In that brief moment is a space that determines our freedom and happiness. We must learn the habit of vetoing temptations as quickly as they come along, or else they will take over.

In this way, perhaps, Jesus overcame his temptations, and we can overcome ours too. We must not think that Jesus had none of these distractions, and we must not assume that his deity made them less appealing or gave him any kind of edge. To do so would be to minimize what it meant for him to be the Son of Man. Instead, we should be encouraged that Christ overcame his temptations, though truly human, and we can thus overcome ours as well.

THE UPSIDE OF TEMPTATION

Still the question remains: Why would God subject Jesus and us to temptation in the first place? And how are we to overcome it?

A few years ago, the Vatican released a study confirming that the sins most often confessed by men are different from those confessed by women.[3] For men, the top three sins are: sex (lust), substance abuse (gluttony), and shirking their responsibilities (sloth). For women, the top three are: condescending or critical spirit (pride), jealousy (envy), and bitterness (anger). In case you wonder whatever happened to the seven deadly sins, they're alive and well. I have no hard data, but from my experiences of praying with people and counseling them over the last thirty years, the Vatican's report seems pretty accurate. I checked a few confessional websites, and it's pretty much the same story. People confess to affairs, substance abuse, stealing, or cheating, and when they write, they seem torn in two by desire and conscience. They want to hold on to the pleasure, yet they want to get rid of the guilt.

That's the way most of us think about temptation. We see it as an assault on our righteousness. It's the Devil inside us. Something dark and sinister. Something to cover up. Something to overcome. There is no winning. There is only resisting. Hopefully, it will pass. And so, when we are tempted, the question we keep asking is, "How can I resist this? How do I stop myself?"

But the story of Jesus' temptation challenges that. If temptation is only a distraction from a good and virtuous life—if it's only a chance to do wrong instead of right, to make something worse instead of better—then you have to wonder why the Holy Spirit sent Jesus into the desert to be tempted. Why did he make Jesus vulnerable to something that couldn't help him, but could only hurt him?

Perhaps there is more to temptation than we think. Maybe temptation is more than a test. Maybe it's a FaultLine—a place of intense pressure, a place we want to avoid but, like the wilderness, a place we need to stay in. Maybe Jesus didn't merely survive the wilderness; maybe he needed it. Maybe he didn't just resist temptation; maybe he leveraged it for something even greater. Luke's gospel seems to bear this out. In the first three chapters, before Jesus was tempted, he was prophesied and conceived by the Spirit (1:35). After he was born, he was confirmed by one who was "moved by the Spirit . . . [to go]

into the temple courts" at the perfect time (2:27). Years later, before anyone knew of Jesus, the most popular evangelist of the day prophesied, "He will baptize you with the Holy Spirit and fire" (3:16), and this led directly to Jesus' own baptism in which "the Holy Spirit descended on him in bodily form like a dove" (3:22). All of this was confirmed when a voice from heaven was heard saying, "You are my Son, whom I love; with you I am well pleased" (3:22). By the end of Luke's third chapter, it is very clear who this person is. He is Christ the Lord (2:11). He is the salvation of God (3:6). He is the Messiah, the one possessed by God's Spirit (3:16). He is the favored one (3:22).

His mission was clear, his path predetermined. From here, he knew exactly what he must do. And because he had to do it in this world—and not in some other—he had to be tempted by this world, and so he "was led by the Spirit into the wilderness, where . . . he was tempted." It was the final stage of his preparation. After the forty days were over, he "returned to Galilee in the power of the Spirit, and news about him spread through the whole countryside" (4:14). He taught in their synagogues (4:15) and told them, "The Spirit of the Lord is on me, because he has anointed me to proclaim good news to the poor. He has sent me to proclaim freedom for the prisoners . . . to set the oppressed free, to proclaim the year of the Lord's favor" (4:18–19).

Have you ever wondered how Jesus' trajectory would have been different without that brief season when he was tempted? What would have happened if he had gone straight from his baptism (3:22) into his preaching (4:15) without that period of temptation in between? No doubt, his preaching would have been just as divine, but would it have been as clear? Would it have had the same authority? Could he have proclaimed freedom for the prisoners if he had not beaten their captor just a few days before? Perhaps those forty days in the wilderness were more crucial to Jesus' success than we think. Maybe they were the place where he began to get traction. Maybe he didn't just protect his ground from the Devil; maybe he took back some ground from the Devil.

What I am saying is that temptation is a contest. There are winners and losers. Whenever we are tempted, two superpowers are vying for our loyalty or for the use of our faculties. At the end of the day, one of them leaves empowered, and the other waits for a more opportune time. We leave the wilderness either stronger or weaker. We are better or worse, but we are never the same. In temptation we are trained for places and things that God has commissioned us to do, and so our preparation occurs, not only in spite of temptation, but in it. Perhaps God's Spirit leads us into the wilderness to be tempted because it is there in the heat of temptation that we steel our resolve against the distractions around us. Perhaps we think God will separate us from all these distractions and the evil around us and when he does, we will finally be holy. Maybe we think that holiness means we are impervious to these things, in our own little world. But in truth, we will never be in our own little world—or if we are, we will not be much good for this one. Being holy is about staying focused in the same world that everyone else is in, with the same distractions and tendencies everyone else has. The Holy Spirit doesn't give us magical powers to resist these things. No, we must learn to resist them, and there is no way to do that except to be in them.

When Tiger Woods was a child, his father knew he would be a special golf player someday, and so he created exercises to develop every aspect of his game. In his book *Playing Through*, he wrote:

By the time Tiger was seven, I realized it was time for me to make sure his mental game was progressing as rapidly as his physical game. So I put him through "Woods Finishing School." I would try to distract Tiger on the golf course by jingling the change in my pocket before he attempted a putt, or I would pump the brakes in the golf cart before his backswing on an iron shot. It was psychological warfare—I did everything with the best intentions, of course. I wanted to make sure he would never run into anybody who was tougher mentally than he was and we achieved that. Eventually, nothing I did to distract him during practice rounds could make the boy flinch or falter. He developed nerves of steel. One time a security marshal's walkie-talkie accidentally kicked on at top volume while Tiger was in the middle of his backswing. Tiger later said that he never heard it. . . . I tried to prepare him as best I could to win. That was the goal.[4]

Tiger's father knew that the world into which he was headed was fiercely competitive and that he would often play in conditions that were less than ideal. If he could not change the conditions his son would play in, at least he could teach him how to stay focused.

Perhaps this is why Jesus was led into the desert to be tempted. Maybe it's why we are led there as well. God is not hoping we will fail—he is not even wondering if we will fail. He simply knows that since we can't eliminate every distraction, we will have to learn to stay focused instead. We will have to learn how to possess ourselves. If we can learn to say "No deal!" to whatever is offered, we will gain the strength of whatever temptation we resist.

WHERE IS YOUR WILDERNESS?

A wilderness is a dry and desolate place, abandoned to the wild and subject to powers beyond our control. When someone in the Bible went into the wilderness, it was never on purpose. People were driven there, left there, or on their way to somewhere else. But it was always against their wishes, and they usually got out of the wilderness as soon as they could. That is, if they got out at all, for the wilderness claimed many victims. Moses called it, "The vast and dreadful wilderness, that thirsty and waterless land, with its venomous snakes and scorpions" (Deut. 8:15). In the wilderness lived the evil spirits and immorality (Jer. 3:2). Into the wilderness the people wandered forty years and were buried in their graves of craving (see Num. 11:34). It was the bane of the psalmist, the exile of prophets, an asylum for the insane, and a prison for deposed kings. If you were in it, you were up against predators—wolves, jackals, lions, and serpents—the forces of nature, and your own raw need. Depending on the season, there was little water and almost no vegetation. It is not surprising, then, that the Devil's first offer was for food: "Tell these stones to become bread," he said (Matt. 4:3). After forty days out there, one would be hungry enough to do it if he could. The temptation was not for Jesus to prove who he was; he didn't need to prove it to the Devil, and no one else was there. The temptation was to seize ahead of time what the Father was planning to give him later. Israel (God's "son") was tempted the same way in the wilderness. Faced with the same temptation, Jesus neither grumbled nor complained, and he didn't presume to usurp the Father's privilege of providing good things for his Son. He chose to be patient and wait, to live on God's promise rather than the bread he could provide for himself. It was a huge wager. There was a lot at stake. There was more to the temptation than food. The Son of God was tempted—as we are—to exchange his trust in the Father's goodness for something he could give himself today. Deal or no deal?

Where is your wilderness? What places seem to be abandoned and wild, subject to forces beyond your control? Where are the dangerous places and what temptations find you there? Quite often, temptation is about turf. There are places, people, and events that tempt us. In their presence, we are more vulnerable to our great weakness. The Devil finds us there and offers us an exchange of something more for something less—deal or no deal. What he offers seems harmless and more appealing than what we hope for or already have.

Such circumstances can act as a "trigger" for temptation. Maybe it's a physical location, like an office or kitchen. Perhaps it's a time of day, like after everyone else has gone to bed. It could be a routine, like a drive through traffic or a regularly scheduled event. Some people are like saints . . . until you put them in charge of something. Suddenly, everything changes. Like a police dog, playful and loving until you put the harness on it, such people can became harsh and insensitive, even cruel when they wear the harness of power. Power is their wilderness, where the evil spirits find them. Sometimes a pattern of behavior, from a child or spouse, can act as a trigger. Sometimes it's just pure fatigue at the end of the week. Whatever it is, every one of us has at least one, and when we find ourselves in that wilderness, the same temptation occurs. If we could get out of it, we might leave it like the desert. We can't. We are stuck there, and as long as we are, we are subject to forces beyond our control.

I used to worry about these seasons of temptation, because I thought they were evidence of something evil lurking in me. I thought that if I was led by the Spirit, I would be free from temptation or at least have magical powers to resist it. If I was holy, how could I be dragged away and enticed by my own evil desires (see James 1:14)? If every time I tried to do good, evil was right there with me, then that was my own fault (see Rom. 7:18–19). But this is only one reason for temptation. There are others. Sometimes we are tempted by our own evil desires, but sometimes we are tempted when the Spirit leads us into our wilderness and calls us to reclaim that place in the power of Jesus' name. Sometimes temptation is a contest between two superpowers who meet to do battle over some place in our lives. We cannot simply resist it. We must fight for it, conquer it, and take back that domain. In the wilderness, anything that does not make us better will make us worse.

TAKING BACK THE DESERT

Most references to the wilderness in the Bible are negative, but there are a few exceptions. Occasionally, God promised to do something outrageous in the wilderness, especially in the book of Isaiah. Again and again, the fiery prophet portrayed salvation as the taking back of the wilderness. "The desert [will become] a fertile field," he said, "and the fertile field [will seem] like a forest" (32:15). "Water will gush forth in the wilderness and streams in the desert. The burning sand will become a pool, the thirsty ground bubbling springs. In the haunts where jackals once lay, grass and reeds and papyrus will grow. And a highway will be there; it will be called the Way of Holiness" (35:6–8). He was talking about reclaiming the wilderness.

Keep reading. It gets better: "I will put in the desert the cedar and the acacia, the myrtle and olive. I will set junipers in the wasteland, the fir and the cypress together, so that people may see and know . . . that the hand of the Lord has done this" (41:19–20). "The Lord will surely comfort Zion. . . . He will make her deserts like Eden, her wastelands like the garden of the Lord" (51:3).

This is profound. When the Spirit leads us into the wilderness to be tempted, he intends for us not just to resist the Tempter, but to reclaim the wilderness for the glory of God. God does not want us to merely survive temptation. He plans to redeem it, to convert our wilderness into a garden and our wasteland into a highway of holiness.

But how? Not long ago, I came across one of those survival books that tell you how to stay alive when you're stranded in the wilderness. It was a sort of "Bear Grylls for Dummies," and so I started leafing through it in case I should ever find myself stranded in an Indiana cornfield with no way out. As the writer said, "You never know when and where you'll find yourself in a survival situation." The book was filled with anecdotes of people who didn't survive and those who did, and one of the main differences between them was how prepared they were before they went into the wilderness. According to the experts, preparation is the key. People who conquer the wilderness have things and know things the rest of us do not. They know that once you are out there, it's too late to figure it out. You are subject to forces beyond your control, so your only chance at beating them, at reclaiming the wilderness, is to go into it prepared. This made me wonder how Jesus survived the wilderness. The question is not so much how he resisted temptation once he was there, but how he prepared for it before he got there. What did he have with him or in him when he entered the wilderness? What did he know that helped him survive? How did he take back the desert?

First, he went in the power of the Holy Spirit: "Jesus, full of the Holy Spirit . . . was led by the Spirit into the wilderness" (Luke 4:1). Instead of reducing this to mere God-talk or a simple act of consecration, we should meditate on what it means to do anything full of the Holy Spirit. For starters, it means that we are not double-minded. We do not have conflicting interests between God and ourselves. We have declared our loyalty to God and God alone. But it also means that we are conscious of it on a daily basis. We have repeatedly reminded ourselves that we are not our own (1 Cor. 6:19). Our bodies belong to the Holy Spirit (3:16). We are the temple of God (2 Cor. 6:16). Those who are full of the Holy Spirit not only know this, but are cognizant of it every day. They make decisions based on this simple fact as though it were a pillar in the middle of their lives. They find out what pleases the Spirit and then bring those things into their daily routines (Eph. 5:10). And they think about this all the time.

People who are full of the Holy Spirit have developed a pattern of yielding to his impulses and constraining their own, until the power and virtue that flows out from them is not something they have manufactured but something they have unleashed. They have found a way to become subdominant in their own lives. They have allowed the Holy Spirit to express his personality in theirs. People who are full of the Spirit are full of love, joy, peace, gentleness, kindness, faith, meekness, and self-control (see Gal. 5:22–23) long before they get into the wilderness.

Too often, we reduce being filled with the Holy Spirit to a simple decision to invite him into our lives. We minimize this life to a sanctifying moment, like baptism, that we think moves us into a different class or gives us magical powers over sin. But to be filled by the ' Spirit we already possess surely means more than this. It is to be controlled by him. It is to walk next to him (Gal. 5:25). It is to talk with him as with any good friend and to allow him to change our minds while we're talking. It is to make ourselves available to do his work.

Before assuming we are already filled with the Spirit—and thus prepared for the wilderness of temptation—we should think hard about what this means and ask ourselves how true it is of us. To be filled with the Holy Spirit is more than a sanctifying moment.

More, but not less. So perhaps the way to start is to pray and to declare again our loyalties to God and his Spirit. If you have never done that, or even if you have, why not do it now? Go ahead, put this book down and talk directly to God.

Another way in which Jesus was prepared for the wilderness had to do with his identity. Two times, the Devil said to him, "If you are the Son of God" (Luke 4:3, 9) as though the matter had not yet been decided. Only days before this, as Jesus was being baptized, "a voice came from heaven: 'You are my Son, whom I love; with you I am well pleased'" (Luke 3:22). As he went into the wilderness, Jesus was armed with the knowledge that he was the Son of God and that the Father was pleased with him. To go back to our metaphor of *Deal or No Deal*, that was the value of the briefcase at his side.

TALKING DUTCH

Not long ago, a young man came to see me with a sin to confess. After he confessed, I asked him why he committed the sin, and his answer surprised me. He said he didn't have a choice. It was as if powers beyond his control took him over and made him commit the sin.

"But how can that be?" I asked. "The sin is too far below you. The power you speak of is so much less than the power within you."

Now he was surprised. He was expecting the usual speech about trying hard to resist an urge that was so natural, but I was telling him that he was working too hard to commit a sin that was unnatural. He was expecting me to say he was having too much fun, but I was telling him he wasn't having enough.

"What do you mean?" he asked. So I borrowed a line from C. S. Lewis: "Our desires are not too strong, but too weak; we are half-hearted creatures, fooling about with drink and sex and ambition when infinite joy is offered us. . . . We are far too easily pleased. . . . Now since we are made for heaven, the desire for our proper place [is] already in us but not yet attached to the true object, and will even appear as a rival of that object."[5]

"If you knew who you were," I said, "you would never stoop for the kind of thing you just confessed. You would live above it because you can."

For a long time he sat there speechless, shaking his head. Then he said, "No one has ever told me that before."

Has someone told you?

Think about it. How many of your temptations are rooted in not knowing who you are? How often are you tempted toward pride or lust because you do not feel significant? You don't know that you are beloved? Or you struggle with greed and envy because you forget that God is a Father who likes to give good things to his children (Luke 11:13).

The Bible gives us many names, and yet we too often ignore them. We are told that God "chose us in him before the creation of the world to be holy and blameless in his sight" or that we are adopted "in accordance with his pleasure and will" (Eph. 1:4–5). We are said to be "marked in him with a seal, the promised Holy Spirit, who is a deposit guaranteeing our inheritance" (1:13–14). In fact, "we are God's handiwork, created in Christ Jesus to do good works, which God prepared . . . us to do" (2:10). We are "fellow citizens" with the very people we most admire (2:19). We are the very "dwelling in which God lives by his Spirit" (2:22). But we forget.

I am convinced that in the final analysis this lies at the bottom of our trouble. We do not know who we are, and so we act like someone else. And the person we imitate is always less than the person we really are. If we could only remember who we are and what is available to us because of our identity as a child of God, we would be more prone to act like it. When Jesus went into the wilderness, he went in with the knowledge of who he was and what was available to him.

It is not enough to merely quote the Scriptures when we are tempted. We must learn to believe the Scriptures before we are tempted, until they become for us the best descriptor of the way things are. It does no good to say, "Man does not live by bread alone," unless one truly believes that the Lord will provide, or that his compassions are new every morning. Scripture is not a lucky charm to keep the

Devil away. Rather, it is a lens through which we see our lives in the world. It is a way of defining reality. The more we grasp the narrative, the wisdom, the penetrating truth of the Bible, the more easily we will see through the lies of temptation. The more we comprehend the message of the Bible, the more we will value the briefcase at our side, the less appealing all the others will seem, and the easier it will be to say, "No deal!"

And once we say it, in the wilderness where we are tempted, God's Spirit will transform that desert into fertile ground. The FaultLine of temptation will produce in us a majestic beauty, until those who see it will say, "The hand of the Lord has done this."

6

A FAILURE

a different kind of perfect

It was Wednesday, June 2, 2010. A twenty-eight-year-old Detroit Tigers pitcher, with an otherwise lackluster career, was on the mound in the top of the ninth inning with his team winning 3–0. There were two outs and no one on base. He had retired the last twenty-six consecutive batters without allowing a hit or even a walk. Half of the outs had been grounders. Armando Galarraga was pitching the perfect game. In baseball, the "perfect game" is one in which the winning pitcher completes the game without allowing a single player from the opposing team to safely reach base. That means no runs, no hits, no walks, no hit batters—nothing but twenty-seven up and twenty-seven down. At the time, only twenty perfect games had been pitched in the last hundred years of Major League baseball.

On a one-ball, one-strike count, shortstop for the Cleveland Indians, Jason Donald, hit a routine ground ball to the right of Tigers first baseman Miguel Cabrera. Cabrera cleanly backhanded the ball and tossed it to Galarraga, who was covering first base. The runner stretched to beat the throw, but the throw beat him by nearly a step, and Donald was called—wait. . . . Safe?

Did the ump just call him safe? Unbelievable!

Veteran umpire James Joyce was and is still widely considered one of the best in the game, but he clearly missed the call that ruined Galarraga's perfect game.

"I felt pretty good when I made the call," said Joyce after the game, "but halfway off the field was the time I knew I probably missed it." Sports fans are famous for saying that something was "obvious" or that "anyone could see it," when it was really quite close. But go ahead and Google it. You can look at it from any angle at any speed, and there is no way you can call that man safe.

In the umpire's dressing room after the game, Joyce asked the attendant to cue up the play. He watched it one time. He's never watched it again. He doesn't need to.

"It was the biggest call of my career," he said, "and I kicked it; I just cost that kid a perfect game." MLB.com said it this way: "The imperfect call spoiled the perfect game."[1] *Sports Illustrated* dubbed it "the most heartbreaking call in baseball history."[2] Having been a Tigers fan all my life, I'm inclined to agree.

What does a guy do when he blows it in front of hundreds of thousands of people? What happened next was extraordinary. Joyce invited reporters into the dressing room and frankly admitted that he missed the call.

"I missed it from here to that wall," he said. "I had a great angle and I missed it. I missed it. I took something away from him, and if I could, I would give it back in a minute." Then he did something almost unprecedented. He asked the reporters to leave the room and for Galarraga to be brought in so Joyce could apologize.

"When I saw him," Galarraga said, "I was like, 'Oh my gosh; he is red like a tomato.' He hugged me right away [and said] not a word." Finally Joyce managed to say in a quivering voice, "*Lo siento*" — I'm sorry — and he started to cry. Galarraga said, "He tried to talk. He'd say a couple words, 'You were perfect; I was not.' I felt so bad [but] I didn't feel bad for me; I felt bad for him."

Later, that night Joyce drove to Toledo, Ohio, where his eighty-six-year-old mother, Ellouise, lives in the three-bedroom, one-bath brick home that Joyce was raised in. As he approached the stoop, he could hear the television blaring in the living room.

"Did you watch the game?" he asked his mom.

"No, I started to," she said, "but I got interested in something else."

"So you haven't heard what happened?"

She was the only one. By that time James Joyce was the hottest search on Google.

"Mom, can you turn that down so I can talk to you?" And when she did, Joyce told her, "Tomorrow, this is going to be all over the airwaves."

When tomorrow came, the story took an even stranger turn. Far from being angry with each other, Galarraga and Joyce became symbols of sportsmanship, as word spread of Joyce's emotional apology and Galarraga's gracious response. That night, Joyce was greeted with applause as he entered the field to umpire again, this time behind home plate. Galarraga was awarded a new Corvette, courtesy of General Motors, and as he handed the official lineup to Joyce before the game, the two embraced again, and again Joyce was moved to tears. They were not enemies. They were new friends.

The following week, *Sports Illustrated* ran a story on the incident and called it "A Different Kind of Perfect." The article said, "It was the epitome of the human element — not so much for the mistake that was made as for the subsequent humility and grace of the two men."[3]

GREATNESS IN FAILURE

Perfect is a Latin term meaning "thorough" or "complete." It means nothing is lacking. Nothing is left undone. But over the last millennium it has come to mean flawless. Impeccable. Unblemished. Ideal. A performance is "perfect" when the performer does everything right and leaves nothing undone. He hits every note. She finishes every move. The lines are right, balanced and symmetrical. Everything is in the right place and the right proportion. The Olympics were the quintessential model for this, back when athletes used to compete for the "perfect ten." Artists, musicians, writers, dancers, even carpenters all strive for this kind of perfection. They want their work to be flawless, precise, full, and elegant.

But perfection has a price. It demands that one be obsessed with one's work. It can cause a chronic dissatisfaction or restlessness and has been linked to many mental health issues including depression, anxiety, obsessive-compulsive disorder, eating disorders, marital problems, workaholism, procrastination, insomnia and even suicide.[4] But sadly enough, the work it produces is often brilliant. We love what perfectionism produces, but we hate what it does to people.

But when it comes to relationships, there's a different kind of perfect. Galarraga's game that night was not flawless. It was tainted with a bad call and scarred by frustration and regret. There was anger, shock, guilt, and profound disappointment. From an umpire's perspective, it was a nightmare, a colossal failure, or what *Sports Illustrated* called "preposterously wrong."[5] And yet, what followed was redemptive, inspiring, and beautiful. What rises from failure can be a kind of perfect that is larger, more epic, more interesting, and more human than something merely flawless. It is perfect, but it is not exact. It is less than ideal. Terribly flawed. And yet, it's a different kind of perfect. It's not perfection in spite of one's flaws. Nor perfection alongside one's flaws. Nor perfection that simply ignores one's flaws. And it's surely not perfection that tolerates one's flaws. No, this different kind of perfect is a perfection that absorbs one's flaws and takes them up into something that is larger and more interesting, something better than a perfect ten.

MAGNIFICENT FAILURES

What happens when you blow it big time? There are lots of examples of this in the Bible.

Think of Moses, who struck the rock instead of speaking to it as God had commanded. He was a reluctant, even weak-kneed, leader with a history of aggravated assault (Ex. 2:11–12). He was often angry and frustrated, even to the point of quitting, and he lacked self-confidence. Yet Moses was called a faithful servant and the writer of Hebrews compared him to Christ himself (see Heb. 3:2–5). In fact, he was called the best leader Israel ever had. Since the day he died, "no prophet has risen . . . like Moses, whom the LORD knew face to face" (Deut. 34:10). Yes, Moses was less than ideal—he was terribly flawed—but he was a different kind of perfect.

Or think of David, anointed king while he was yet a boy. By age twelve, he had killed a lion, bear, and ten-foot giant. And by the end of his twenties, he'd written many psalms and rescued the ark of the covenant from Philistines. He was a prodigy and king of a rapidly emerging nation. And then there was that awful night when he risked it all for an affair with Bathsheba. Within a few weeks, her husband had been killed and David had taken Bathsheba as his wife. There is no doubt that David's decisions cost him terribly. He lost something he never quite got back. But David also genuinely repented and became the model of a good king. In fact, David was considered the ideal king, and Christ himself is called the "Son of David." David was far from innocent. But he was a different kind of perfect.

Perhaps the best example is Peter. When first called by Jesus, Peter quickly dropped everything and followed. He was "all in." But he failed to calculate what it would cost him. Peter could be strong in the moment, but he was often unprepared for what came next. The night Jesus walked on water is a case in point. While the other disciples were cowering in the boat, Peter yelled out, "Lord . . . tell me to come to you on the water." So Jesus said, "Come." And immediately Peter began to walk on the water toward Jesus. It was his finest moment. Then, only a minute later, "when he saw the wind, he was afraid, and, beginning to sink, cried out" (Matt. 14:28–30).

This was typical Peter. His best and worst moments were often the same.

The same pattern occurs only two chapters later (Matt. 16). When Jesus asked, "Who do you say I am?" Peter blurted out, "You are the Messiah," and when he said it, Jesus called him the "rock." It was another fine moment. But a minute later, when Peter told Jesus he couldn't go to the cross, the "rock" became a "stumbling block" (16:23). This is the way it went with Peter. His best and worst moments were often close together.

Toward the end of Jesus' life, Peter once again made rash promises: "Lord, I am ready to go with you to prison and to death" (Luke 22:33). When Jesus corrected him, saying that Peter would actually deny him three times, Peter interrupted and insisted, "Even if all fall away . . . I will never disown you" (Mark 14:29, 31).

Like Peter, most of us are wired for failure. We overestimate our loyalty, potential, or intellect. We consistently rate ourselves "above average," even though we know, mathematically speaking, that 50 percent of us are below average. Most of us say we are "better than average" drivers, students, lovers, or leaders.

One study surveyed over one million high schools students and found that 100 percent of them rated themselves as "above average" students. Sixty percent rated themselves in the top 10 percent, and 25 percent put themselves in the top 1 percent. When asked what kind of leader they would be, only 2 percent said they were "below average."[6] And where do they get these delusions of grandeur?

Well, from their teachers and parents, of course. Ninety-four percent of our college professors say they do "above average" work, and, depending on the survey, between 30 and 40 percent of our professionals say they are in the top 5 percent. This is the equivalent of saying, "Even if all fall away . . . I will never disown you." We consistently rate ourselves a little better, a little smarter, and a little more devout than everyone else.

Most of us are legends in our own minds. And with these kinds of fantasies, you can imagine how hard it is for us to fail. But we do. We get cut from the team. We get passed over for the promotion. We apply for the job but don't get hired, or we get laid off. Our thesis gets rejected. Our grant gets denied. Our business goes bankrupt. We get turned down for grad school.

Failure is always hard on us, but when it has a moral component, it is crippling. It challenges us at the core. The conservative woman gets divorced. The Christian man loses his job because they found porn on his computer. The pastor's son runs away from home. The coach of the Christian school is arrested for DUI. The teacher is caught cheating on the standardized tests. These are not just failures. They are stark denials of what is in our core.

A FAULTLINE OF GRACE

Failure is a FaultLine. We experience friction and heat because the foundations of our lives are moving. Sometimes we fail because we have done something wrong. But just as often we fail and have done nothing wrong. It just happens. We are subject to forces beyond our control. We would never wish ourselves to be in such a place, but sooner or later every one of us will fail and, more often than we like to admit, we will blow it big time. Like every other FaultLine, failure will make us either better or worse. It all depends . . . but not on the failure itself. Rather, it depends on what comes next.

The key to redeeming our failure is how we handle the aftermath. It is essential that we do the right thing after we have done the wrong thing. The trouble is that we are wired to do the wrong thing twice. We like to cover it up. To avoid it. To minimize it because we want to protect our fragile egos at a time when they are most vulnerable.

When we are caught in the FaultLine of failure, we feel torn in two directions. Part of us wants to deny it and run. And part of us wants to admit it or give in to it and throw everything away.

When we fail, we are tempted to ask, "Why did it happen? Why did I do it?" We think that to explain the failure is to somehow be on top of it instead of under it. It is to distance ourselves from it, as though we were mere observers instead of victims. It implies that we knew better, that we'll get it the next time. If we know why we got rejected or why we got let go, we don't feel quite as helpless. And if the reason we give is someone else's fault, all the better.

But the real trouble lies not in our answers, but in the question. The question at the core of every failure is not "Why did I do it?" but rather "Is grace enough?" And our failures will never help us until we are able to answer yes.

We are fond of speaking or singing about grace, and yet we are so often unable to live with it, because grace implies that we might not be all we think. It means maybe it's not that easy to live with us, that we don't always do what we intend, that our flaws are more trouble-some than we think. When we fail, we require grace—from God, from each other, from the body of Christ, even from the world. We want to live without needing grace. We want to be loved, admired, respected, appreciated—but we do not want to feel graced, because grace reinforces the idea that we are flawed.

The result is that when we fail, we run away from grace, and we have two ways of doing it. These two ways are opposite each other, and depending on our personality, we are more prone to one than the other. But if the one doesn't work, then we will run like mad into the other. Back and forth we go, from one escape to the other, sometimes for years, because we cannot live with grace.

One way to avoid grace is to say we don't need it. There are lots of ways to do this. For instance, think about the last time you blew it. Maybe it was something really big and embarrassing. Or maybe it was rather small, and you kept it to yourself. Maybe you denied or minimized it by saying you didn't really fail because you weren't trying. Maybe you said you didn't care or it didn't count. Maybe you said you weren't embarrassed, because, after all, "lots of people" do what you did. Or maybe you blamed something or someone else. You explained that it wasn't your fault or that the other person's response was way overblown. And the trouble is that you were probably partly right. There usually are good reasons for doing whatever you did—and some of them are truly beyond your control—but you are still seeing the failure from your own perspective rather than the perspective of those who have to live with you. Hannah More, a contemporary of John Wesley, put it like this: "We are eager to blame others without knowing their motives; [and] we are just as eager to vindicate ourselves, even though we cannot be entirely ignorant of our own [motives]"[7]

And have you noticed that while we are using these tactics to avoid needing grace, our lives have not gotten any better? We have not gained strength over the sin that besets us. We have not improved our character, acquired more virtue, or become part of something larger than our lives. And do you know why? Because we cannot live with grace. We prefer innocence to grace. We want to be flawless. Unblemished. Impeccable. A perfect ten. Only everyone knows that we're not . . . Everyone, that is, except us.

Now all that is left to us is grace. And all that grace can give us is a different kind of perfect.

The other way to avoid grace is to act like we deserve it. There are lots of ways to do this, too, but the most common is to pay it back. Sometimes, when we fail, we smother it with promises that we won't do it again. We over-discipline ourselves or even punish ourselves by sabotaging any success or pleasure we might have. I have counseled people who were ruining their second marriage because they still felt guilty for something they did in their first marriage. I have seen people withhold from their new company because of something they did when they were with their last company. They are trying to atone for something they did in their past, because if they can pay it back, they will feel like they deserve the grace they're getting today.

Failure is a FaultLine that makes us better or worse, but we can't get better without grace. Whenever we fail—and we can be sure we will—everything will rise or fall on what we do with grace.

That is exactly where Peter found himself the night he denied Jesus. The Bible says he "went outside and wept bitterly" (Luke 22:62). He was in the middle of a FaultLine. He was directly responsible, and yet it was not premeditated. It must have felt like he was played by forces that were beyond his control. He would never have put himself in this situation, and yet there was no one to blame but himself. From this moment forward, Peter would be defined by this tragic night, or he would be defined by what came next.

Let's pick up the story there.

PETER'S RETURN

The disciples were out fishing all night, and they had gotten skunked. Suddenly, a man standing on the shore spotted them and shouted, "Hey, friends, you haven't caught anything, have you?"

"No," they mumbled, and their voices carried across the waters. The man on the shore was smiling now, like he knew them.

"Cast your nets on the other side," he said, "and there will be plenty."

Really? The man was a hundred yards away. How did he know where the fish were? But he seemed so sure. So the men threw their nets on the other side, and as soon as they did, they felt the familiar drag on their nets and started hauling the fish into their boat.

Apparently, John put things together and recognized the man on the shore as Jesus. "It's the Lord," he said, and immediately Peter jumped into the sea and started swimming. It was another great moment for Peter. The last time he saw Jesus, it was on the heels of his third denial, and now Jesus was back. He was standing on the shore, calling them "friends."

By the time Peter got to shore, he was exhausted, and the rest of his crew were right behind him in the boat. But instead of running up to Jesus and embracing him, they drew back because Jesus had already started "a fire with burning coals" like the one that was going the night Peter betrayed him (see John 18:18). It was as though Jesus was reenacting the scene. There was an awkward silence. Was Jesus still angry? Was he setting a trap? Was he trying to say, "You blew it!" We often see this moment as a great reunion, but that's not exactly the way it was. There was a tentative, almost nervous mood as Jesus welcomed them around the fire. Peter's best moment was beginning to feel like his worst again.

Finally, Jesus broke the silence: "Bring some of the fish you've just caught." So Peter backed away from the fire—never taking his eyes off Jesus—and started unpacking the nets. Then Jesus spoke again.

"Come and have breakfast," he said. What a remarkable thing to say. In the days of the New Testament, a person only ate with his closest friends. Food was scarce, so a person never wasted it on mere acquaintances. To eat with someone was a social event. It was a way of posturing oneself favorably toward another individual. This is why the Pharisees accused Jesus of eating with sinners and tax collectors (Mark 2:15–16). It signaled his acceptance of them. It proved that he wanted to be their friend. So when Jesus invited his disciples—and especially Peter—to breakfast, it was his way of saying, "I am not angry with you; I still love you and I want to be your friend." The Last Supper had become their first breakfast. The night when Peter wept bitterly had been overcome by the morning, and a new day lay ahead of them.

But the matter was far from over. While they were eating, they didn't use each other's names. Isn't that odd? Peter was eating across from the person he had abandoned, and neither was using the other's name. The conversation was polite but guarded, as though between intimate strangers. The mood was tense. Surely, Jesus remembered Peter's failure, but neither one mentioned it.

Finally, when breakfast was over, Jesus broke the silence again, and this time he got right to the point.

"Simon, son of John," he said, and he hadn't called Peter that since the first day they met. "Do you truly love me more than these?" In their last conversation, Peter had boasted, "Even if all fall away, I will not" (Mark 14:29).

Peter knew exactly what he meant, and so, not wanting to make any more rash promises, he simply said, "Yes, Lord . . . you know that I love you." And Jesus said, "Feed my sheep."

What did he say? Wasn't he going to bring it up? Wasn't he going to ask Peter why he did it? Or how he knew that he wouldn't do it again? Three times he asked him, "Do you love me?" and three times Peter said that he did, but neither had mentioned the failure.

How could Peter love him when he still hated himself? But Jesus did not take away the question, because it was the only way back to a different kind of perfect. We can be sorry without actually loving the person we hurt. But we will never love them without being sorry that we hurt them. So this was the thing Jesus wanted to know: "Do you love me?" There is no question more fundamental than this. Until it is answered from the heart, there is no going forward, because love and not penance is the way to be perfect. Penance only evens the score. But love accepts what we cannot pay back and moves us, with our blemishes and scars, toward a different kind of perfect.

HOW TO LIVE WITH GRACE

Some years later, Peter wrote to a multitude of exiles scattered all over the Roman provinces and told them to be strong in the Fault-Line. They would suffer through no fault of their own, he said, and it might tear them up inside and make them want to give in, but if they would only be strong, "the God of all grace" would "make [them] perfect" (1 Pet. 5:10 KJV), only the word he used is not the usual word for perfect. It is a different kind of perfect. It doesn't mean "finished" or "flawless," as in the perfect ten. It means to be whole, with all the necessary components. It refers to the state of being equipped for a task. In Ephesians, it refers to the preparation of the church for becoming perfect, but it does not refer to perfection itself (4:12), at least not in the absolute sense. One scholar says that it has "not so much a qualitative meaning as a functional one."[8] Something is perfect only as it corresponds to the grace given.

Jesus said, in essence, "I know you've failed . . . and maybe you've failed in the worst possible way, but your failure can be the beginning of a different kind of perfect." You will always have a past. Your story will be less than ideal. But God can use your failure and make it part of something that is larger, more interesting, and more human than something merely flawless.

TALKING DUTCH

Maybe you're still tied to some failure in the past, still beating yourself up for something you've done, still living on the treadmill of performance, still trying to make it up to someone or even yourself. Would you be open to some frank advice from Peter?

First, own up to your failure. "'God opposes the proud but shows favor to the humble.' Humble yourselves [accept your humble status], therefore, under God's mighty hand" (1 Pet. 5:5–6). You are wired, like Peter, to overestimate your loyalty. And you are wired to underestimate your failure. If you deny it, minimize it, or blame it on someone else, you are running away from grace. Grace is like financial aid—the more assets you claim at the beginning, the less of it you get in the end. When you posture yourself as anything but poor, you are talking yourself out of grace. If you say it wasn't your fault or wasn't that bad, you are walking out of grace instead of into it. And if you walk out of grace, you cannot be perfect. You can only be flawless, but you're not. So, when you fail, own up to it and admit all of it. Don't hide the details because you think it is too embarrassing to reveal them. You don't have to tell everything to everybody, but you'd better tell everything to somebody. Because in the end, it is never our sins that undo us but the apparatus that we build up around them, to protect them, that does the greatest harm. It's the way we gradually lower our expectations because "nobody's perfect." Or it's the lengths to which we go to justify ourselves or the way we seal off certain areas of our lives from the inquiry of others, even those closest to us. These are the real damages of our sin. So be proactive. Be forthright in your confessions. If you only admit to what others have already found out, it only makes it harder to believe in you again. Accept your humble status. That is, accept the consequences of your sin and the limitations that come with them.

Second, stay in the body. You'll be tempted, almost immediately, to withdraw from your community because of shame masquerading as justice. You'll say that something is unfair, that those people have no right to judge you, or that they have no right to treat you like this. And you're probably right. In fact, every community has problems that are at least as severe as your own. The community's authority over you is not something they deserve; it is something they are given, because there is just no other way for you to be healed except by being with them. They are leading you through the process, not because they are better than you, but simply because that's the role they've been given by God. You have to stay in the body you've offended. You may need someone to broker that for you, or you may need a brief time away, but ultimately you must be healed in the body you've offended.

Third, entrust yourself to God. Peter said, "Cast all your anxiety on him" (1 Pet. 5:7). The word Peter used for anxiety means "to be torn in two directions." Jesus used it to describe someone who was interested in the kingdom of God, but just as interested in the things of this world (Matt. 13:22). So part of you wants to hide, and part of you wants to quit. You have conflicting interests. Take these things back to God and admit them. Then leave your healing up to him. Do not presume to know what is fair or wise. Don't create your own standards or timetable. Leave the timing up to God. The wisdom of God is embodied in those he has put around you, however uninformed they may seem. When you argue with them, don't presume that your only problem is your failure. It isn't. Your real problem is often what comes next—in your presumption, your impatience, or your independent and contrary spirit. If you're not careful, you'll start playing yourself against the body, and if you do, your failure will seem relatively small compared to the problem in your spirit a few months from now. Listen to me, I beg you: "The God of all grace . . . will himself restore you and make you firm and steadfast" (5:10) but you must not abort the process with ideas from your own mind.

Finally, discipline yourself. Peter said, "Be alert and sober of mind. Your enemy the devil prowls around like a roaring lion looking for someone to devour" (5:8). Too many of us have somehow come to believe that the most spiritual people among us are not those who resist sins but those who confess them. The preacher or counselor who stands up and confesses to this or that passion is considered a virtual giant among us. But here we are told to "discipline" ourselves and to "resist" the Devil (vv. 8–9 NRSV). As you recover, remember this: The goal is not to make you a more honest sinner, but to make you a more transparent saint, who, having learned from your failures is ready to move past them. Your sins are not helping you if you keep committing them. The only sins that help you are the ones you get over, not the ones you keep confessing. So you must discipline yourself to resist those things that caused you to fail in the first place. This means that as a result of your failure, there may be places you can no longer go, at least for now. There may be movies you cannot watch or music you cannot listen to. There are probably routines you cannot keep or liberties you cannot enjoy—not because they're wrong in themselves—but because they leave you vulnerable in the place where you once failed. It might help you to sit down with a trusted friend or counselor and work through the routines or habits that once led to your downfall and to think about alternative pathways for your new life.

When I was a child, my parents would often entertain their friends on a Sunday afternoon, and sometimes those conversations required that the children be absent from the room. I never knew what my parents were talking about, but I knew I wasn't supposed to bother them when my mother would hand me and my two sisters a bag of old crayons and a few sheets of paper and tell us to draw them a picture.

As I remember, we would sit down at the kitchen table and start working on our masterpieces, when suddenly, as though possessed by a gremlin, my sister would snatch a crayon and make a random mark on my sheet of paper. I couldn't believe it. There I was, halfway done with a masterpiece that would make Michelangelo jealous, and my sister—she must have been envious of my work—decided to wreck it. I screamed bloody murder. But she just giggled, like her picture was better than mine. So I decided to appeal.

Risking trouble, I would barge into my parents' meeting, with picture in hand, sobbing while I showed them the damage. I was sure my dad would dismiss himself and go settle the score. But instead, he studied my drawing, looked at the mark my sister had made, and said, "Make it a tree."

"What?"

"She used a brown crayon," he said, "so you can make it into a tree."

I couldn't believe it. I didn't barge into his meeting for a lesson in art. I came to get justice. He was telling me to make the damage into part of my picture, but I wanted him to go get my sister and do a little damage of his own.

"But I don't want that mark in there," I said, and he just smiled.

"Well, there it is. Now what are you going to do with it? I suggest you make it a tree."

So I went back to the kitchen and made my little tree. But I waited for an opportune time to get a little vengeance of my own. And when my sister wasn't looking, I snatched a crayon and put a nasty mark on her picture.

Now it was her turn. She jumped up and ran into my parents' meeting, sobbing that I had just ruined her picture. And my dad did the same thing. He studied it and said, "Make it a sun. He used a yellow crayon, and he put it high on the page. You need a sun anyway, so make it a ṣun."

Back and forth we went, from damage to redemption, until little by little we had finished our drawings.

At the end of the day, we brought our pictures to our parents and, do you know what they did? They both smiled and said, "These are beautiful. They're just perfect."

And maybe they were. But they were a different kind of perfect.

Even if our failures form new limitations and even if they cannot be expunged from our past, God can make them into something that is larger and more beautiful than the mark that we, or others, have made on our lives. God himself can restore us with strength and humility, with quietness and confidence, in the very place where we have once failed. Yes, it takes time, and we will have to submit to the process, but God is faithful and he will do it.

7

A SUCCESS

the bad luck of good fortune

N othing succeeds or fails like success.

Jack Whittaker, fifty-five years old and president of his own contracting firm, stopped one night to buy a ticket for the state's lottery, worth 315 million dollars. The next day, when the winning numbers were revealed, Jack was disappointed to learn he was off by only one number. "No surprise," he said. "I never win anything."

A day later, on Christmas Eve, he heard that the numbers had been misreported, and when he checked his ticket again, he found he'd hit the jackpot. Suddenly, the guy who never won anything had won everything—the whole jackpot, all to himself.

Jack claimed the one-time cash option of 170 million dollars and, after the government took its part, went home 113 million dollars richer. "From now on," he thought, "everything will be different." And he was right.

For better or worse.

A religious man, Jack promptly tithed the first eleven million dollars to Christian charities and then set up the Jack Whittaker Foundation, which clothes and feeds low-income families in rural West Virginia. He returned to the store where he bought the winning ticket and gave the clerk a new house, a new Dodge Ram truck, and fifty thousand dollars in cash. He bought himself a new Hummer. He bought his favorite granddaughter, Brandi, a new Corvette and promised her an allowance of two thousand dollars a week.

That's when the trouble began.

Brandi adored her boyfriend Jess. She used her allowance to buy him everything, and before long, the two of them were getting into drugs. One night, Jess ended up dead, face down in one of Whittaker's empty houses—an overdose of cocaine, the coroner said—and when Brandi heard it, she spiraled into depression. Three months later, Brandi too was discovered dead, wrapped in a plastic tarp and dumped behind an abandoned van in a place called Scary Creek.

To cope with his sorrows, Jack took to drinking—while driving—and it didn't take long for the police to notice. One night he rammed his Hummer into a concrete embankment, totaling the vehicle, and when the officer tried to give him a Breathalyzer, Jack refused and was promptly arrested. In court, he erupted, accusing them of trying to convict him of something he didn't do. Wanting to dull the pain, he frequented a strip club called the Pink Pony, and one night, while he was getting drunk, thieves broke into his car and ran off with a suitcase carrying over 545 thousand dollars. When police asked him why he was carrying so much cash, he snapped, "Because I can."

You've probably heard the phrase "A fool and his money are soon parted." In just four years, Jack began to run out of money, so he tried to make it back by gambling. A couple months later, he was sued by Caesars Atlantic City for bouncing 1.5 million dollars in checks to cover his losses.

"I wish I'd have torn that ticket up," he told ABC's Martin Bashir. "I don't know where it will end, but I just know that I don't like Jack Whittaker. I don't like the hard heart I've got. I don't like what I've become."[1]

Neither did his wife. A couple months after the interview, she divorced him — after forty-two years of marriage.

The Oxford scholar of five hundred years ago, Robert Burton said, "If adversity hath killed his thousands, prosperity hath killed his ten thousands [and] therefore, adversity is to be preferred."[2] He said that adversity instructs but prosperity deceives. Adversity makes us miserably happy and prosperity makes us happily miserable.

Most of us would think Burton is an Eeyore. We would love to be happily miserable, at least for a while. But maybe Burton had a point. Prosperity is volatile. Dangerous. Sociologist Paul Schervish says, "Money is like fire; it will warm your feet or it will burn your socks off."[3] Recent studies have shown that those who run suddenly into prosperity suffer from it almost as much as they enjoy it.[4] Those who value being rich are twice as likely to have difficulty forming close friendships and one and a half times as likely to abuse substances, to have trouble concentrating, to fear the negative evaluation of others, and to be emotionally flat-lined.[5] Prosperity, or good fortune, is a FaultLine that makes us better or worse, but we do not always see this because, unlike other FaultLines, we don't usually want to escape good fortune. We want to stay in it.

MOST LIKELY TO SUCCEED

Three areas where we are likely to feel this good fortune are in our possessions, power, and popularity. Possessions increase when we suddenly inherit a lot of money, for example. Power increases when we improve our rank, get promoted, or win an election. Popularity increases when we are recognized or discovered. Sometimes all three increase at once. Most of us desire and even pursue an increase in at least one of these areas. We want a raise, more authority, or to be famous because we underestimate how precarious this FaultLine can be.

Recent studies, in both the US and the UK, have shown that those who suddenly receive money (or possessions) experience dramatic changes, sometimes for the better and sometimes not. According to the research, a significant number of those who win the lottery or inherit a vast sum of money "go on eventually to exhibit better psychological health . . . their mental well-being vastly improved."[6] Many indicate that there is a strong tie between their good fortune and their happiness up to certain point—usually around seventy-five thousand dollars. Beyond that, there is almost no connection until another point—usually around two hundred thousand dollars—after which money actually detracts from their happiness. The difference is not in what people do with their money but in what their money does to them. Robert Frank, a senior editor at *The Wall Street Journal* who studied the impact of wealth upon happiness, wrote that a sudden increase in wealth does not create for us a new situation but only exaggerates our current situation. "If you're unhappy or bad with money and surrounded by people you don't trust," he writes, "then money will only make those problems worse. But if you're fulfilled, careful with money and enjoy a life of strong relationships, the lottery could make things better."[7]

Those who suddenly run into power find themselves in a similar place. Now their opinions matter. People respect them, fear them, or need them, and people want to please them. Over time they learn it's easier to just call for something than to argue for it. They're tempted to think they know best, that their ideas are better, their stories more interesting. They may take credit for work others have done. Or they may take vengeance on those who oppose them.

But there are some who use power to promote or encourage other people. They handle the petty things so that the people who work for them can do the fun and interesting things. The difference is not so much in what they do with their power, but in what their power has done to them. Years ago, when my father was a police chaplain, he traveled with the canine unit. He was surprised to see how peaceful and playful the police dogs were, and so he asked if he could pet them. "Sure," said the officer, "but not when they have the harness on." When they wear the harness, the officer explained, the dogs are all business. They have no play, no friends, no loyalties to anyone except their master. They are defensive and even mean. "Power is like a harness," my father used to say. "It makes us servants or masters, better or worse. But we are never the same."

Those who suddenly become popular or famous also live on the FaultLine of favor. When Roger Waters of the famous rock band Pink Floyd recently described the band's breakup in 1985, he blamed their sudden popularity as the primary reason. Just prior to the release of their album *Dark Side of the Moon*, Waters said the band was reasonably generous with each other. But once they achieved a measure of success, once they did what they set out to do, from then on it was really about clinging to the trademark in a kind of frightened way, not wanting to lose.[8] This is all too common among people whose work has suddenly been discovered. They don't want to let their audience down. They don't want to disappoint others, so they try to perpetuate their success by recreating the thing that made them successful in the first place. They give more attention to their audience and their image than to their craft. But others respond differently. They loan their credibility to others. Or raise the public awareness about a certain cause. Or use their notoriety to connect those who have needs with those who have power to help them. Once more, the difference is in what their popularity does to them.

Most of us come by our favor the old-fashioned way: We earn it. It happens to us slowly. It builds over time. It is more closely and clearly connected to things like our ambition, talent, creativity, or risk. So when we go to explain it, we do so in these terms. We talk about what we did to succeed. We mention hard work, perseverance, and skill. And we are not wrong. But we are only half right. The truth is that good fortune is just as hard to explain as bad luck. There are always reasons, but the reasons themselves do not tell the whole story. There must be another explanation for our fortune.

WHERE DOES GOOD FORTUNE COME FROM?

There are many examples in the Bible of people running into good fortune. None of them saw it coming. It ruined some and helped others. In every instance, the sequence of the stories is the same. First, one in charge bestows good favor on a servant. In other words, the servant is given something he did not earn. Even if the servant has been shrewd and worked hard, his hard work could not explain all the good he received. Next, the servant must decide how he will use it, for better or worse. This is usually done in the absence of the one who is in charge. Finally, the person in charge returns to assess and judge the servant's motives and work.

Luke's parable of the rich farmer is an example.

The ground of a certain rich man yielded an abundant harvest. He thought to himself, "What shall I do? I have no place to store my crops." Then he said, "This is what I'll do. I will tear down my barns and build bigger ones, and there I will store my surplus grain. And I'll say to myself, 'You have plenty of grain laid up for many years. Take life easy; eat, drink and be merry.'" But God said to him, "You fool! This very night your life will be demanded from you." (Luke 12:16–20)

Another example can be found in Jesus' parable of the talents (or Luke's version of the minas). A master, getting ready to go on a journey, called in three of his servants and entrusted what he owned to them (Matt. 25:14–30; Luke 19:12–27). He doled it out in the form of "talents," or stacks of money that equaled about one thousand dollars per talent. The first servant received five stacks, about five thousand dollars, which was the wage of an ordinary worker for about fifteen years. In other words, he won the lotto. The next servant was handed two stacks, about two thousand dollars, which was about seven times his annual salary. The third servant got one stack, about three times his salary, so he still had plenty to work with. But wait. There was a reason for the difference in the servants' fortunes. The master gave to each of them "according to his ability" (Matt. 25:15). This was not luck after all. There was something intentional, though unknown to the servants, about the way they came into their money. They didn't earn it. They didn't win it. It was assigned to them. There were no strings attached, but you can bet the master had expectations. He calculated each servant's ability and assigned them their fortune accordingly.

But how did he know? What was he looking for? Matthew never says. But Luke says that the master was going on a journey "to have himself appointed king" (Luke 19:12). So when he called his servants and gave them the money, he told them, "Put this money to work . . . until I come back" (19:13). After he was made king, he "returned home. Then he sent for the servants . . . in order to find out what they had gained" (19:15). Some scholars argue that this is a poor translation. For starters, the phrase "put this money to work until I come back" is better translated, "do business with this until I come again."[9] Further, the word for "gained" is rare in the New Testament, and it means to do business or to earn through trading. Some translate it "to fully occupy oneself." So the question posed by the master is not "How much have you gained by trading?" but "How fully have you been occupied?" New Testament scholar Kenneth Bailey explains the difference: "If the master wants to find out what has been gained . . . he will ask some form of 'Show me the money.' But if he's asking, 'How much business have you transacted?' he is seeking to discover the extent to which they have openly and publicly declared their loyalty to him during the risky period of his absence."[10] Perhaps this is why the master ignored their profit and pointed directly to their faithfulness: "Well done, good and *faithful* servant!" he said (Matt. 25:21, emphasis added). To be faithful, then, does not mean to produce more but to invest in something the master believes in, in something the master will do when he returns.

When the third servant came to reckon, he was in a different mood. While the first two servants were invited to "share your master's happiness," this servant saw only his obligation. There was no happiness to be had for him. From the moment he was given the money, he saw only his duty. He saw a standard and a deadline. He could not enjoy the master's favor because he was stuck with it. For him, the master's return was like judgment day, and I wonder if this was at the core of his trouble. He had a fundamentally different and twisted view of the master as a hard man who always got something from nothing. "I was afraid," he said, "and went out and hid your gold in the ground. See, here is what belongs to you" (Matt. 25:25). The last line—"here is what belongs to you"—is actually an old Jewish colloquialism that means something like "I am not responsible for this."[11]

The third servant was ruled by two evils that tyrannize many who run into good fortune. One is an obligation to produce more, and the other is the fear of losing what they already have. This poor man was torn between them. He couldn't possess the master's favor without feeling obligated to earn even more of it. And yet, if he tried to produce more of it, he risked losing what little he had. So he buried it because he couldn't handle the pressure that comes with being favored. Think of it. Isn't this a terrible way to handle good fortune?

Wouldn't it be better to give both obligation and fear back to the master? After all, the reason we've been favored in the first place is not simply so we can share in the master's work, but so that we can share in his *happiness*. Perhaps he wants us to share not just the load, but the joy that comes with doing the master's work. This is a fundamentally different kind of master.

THE FAULTLINE OF GOOD FORTUNE

In the contrast between the servants we can see the FaultLine of good fortune. Imagine how the servants felt when they were assigned their talents. Each of them saw a sudden, unexpected, undeserved increase in their possessions. By the time they left the master's office, their hearts were racing. When the first two servants got home, they must have felt a little like Jack Whittaker, coming through the door and shouting, "Honey, I just hit the jackpot."

In some ways, they did. All three saw their income go up. Even the third servant received three times the amount he could make in a year. In our currency today, that's almost two hundred thousand dollars, which is the average sum of inheritance in the US. All three started with a tremendous advantage, though in differing degrees. All three were told to "put this to work." All three were suddenly on a FaultLine. From there, they went in opposite directions.

Two of them got better, one of them got worse, but none of them stayed the same. For two, the good fortune was an advantage. For the third, it was bad luck. For two it was an opportunity: "The master trusts us; we cannot lose." For the third, it was an obligation: "The master has high expectations; I cannot win." Two of them tried to leverage it, while the other tried to protect it. Two were motivated by favor, and the other was motivated by fear. All of them felt the privilege and the responsibility of the master's order to "put this to work." But for two of them, the privilege outweighed the responsibility; and for the other, the responsibility outweighed the privilege. Two of them felt blessed, while the other felt stuck. By the end of the story, the point is clear: Favor is a FaultLine that makes us either better or worse.

Success is not something we earn, not a mere consequence of things we have done; it's something we're given. Success is something that has been entrusted to us no matter how hard we've had to work for it. It is favor more than reward. Even though it often follows discipline, sacrifice, and hard work, there seems to be no ratio between how hard a person works and the amount of success he or she enjoys. There's a pattern, to be sure, but it's never exact and it's not guaranteed. Favor implies that someone loves us, that they believe in us, and that they want us to share in their happiness. The most important thing about anyone who succeeded in the Bible was that they were favored. Abraham was. Jacob was. Moses was. Samuel, David, Solomon, Esther, and Daniel were, and this is always the first reason given for their success. They worked hard, and sometimes they did heroic things. But the most common reason given for their exploits is that "the Lord was with them." It's true that successful people have often formed the habit of doing things that failures don't like to do. But success is more complicated than that. We can say that it follows certain behaviors, but the link between those behaviors and success is more circumstantial than we like to think. What the parable of the talents teaches us is that long before we succeed, the master has calculated what we are capable of managing, and he has assigned it by wrapping it in things like coincidence, momentum, chance, even luck. However we get it, we are stewards, not owners, and "the task of a steward," says Gordon MacDonald, "is simply to manage something for the owner until the owner comes to take it back."[12]

Our primary role in managing good fortune is to invest it in things the Master will do when he returns. Our task is not to become more successful—or rich, or powerful, or prominent—and not even to protect what fortune we already have. Our task is to invest it, while we have it, in things that interest God. We must be careful to avoid the two evils that spoil good fortune: the obligation to produce more and the fear of losing what we have already have. Instead, we must ask, "Where would the Master put this if he were here to invest it himself?" The joy that comes with doing the Master's work is the fringe benefit of investing his favor into things he enjoys doing. The amount we gain may vary, but our task is always the same: "Put this [favor] to work until I come back" (Luke 19:13).

HOW TO SURVIVE GOOD FORTUNE

But how do we put favor to work? How do we know what the Master would invest in? One way to know is to examine the lives of those in the Bible who came unexpectedly into favor. What did *they* do? Who or what did they invest in, and what was the result?

One example is in the life of Joseph. One of twelve boys, Joseph was favored from the beginning. From the moment we are introduced to him in Genesis, we are told that his father "loved Joseph more than any of his other sons" (37:3). More than a casual reference to Jacob's bias, this is a sign of things to come. For the next thirteen chapters of Genesis, we read repeatedly how Joseph was favored in spite of his trouble and how, more than anything else, this favor was the reason for his success. Joseph's life was hard and unfair. He was beaten and left for dead by his brothers (37:17–20). Then later he was sold as a slave (37:25–28). He was falsely accused of rape by Potiphar's wife and promptly sent to prison without a trial (39:6–20). Once in prison, he was befriended by another prisoner who had connections to the pharaoh, but he was soon forgotten once the prisoner was released (40:23). Two more years passed before Joseph was heard from again (41:1). In all, it was twenty long years before Joseph's life would begin to turn around, and none of the trouble he experienced in those first twenty years was his own fault.

But if we slow down and read his story more carefully, we'll notice another theme woven throughout Joseph's trouble. From the first sign of trouble, "the LORD was with Joseph so that he prospered" even while he suffered the injustices (39:2). For instance, when he was beaten and sold as a slave, "the Lord gave him success in everything he did, [and] Joseph found favor in [Potiphar's] eyes" (39:3–4). When he was sent to prison without a trial, the Lord "showed him kindness and granted him favor in the eyes of the prison warden. So the warden put Joseph in charge of all those held in prison" (39:21–22). And when he was forgotten in prison, God interrupted Pharaoh with a dream that only Joseph could interpret, and then opened the door for Joseph to interpret the dream. When he did, the pharaoh was overwhelmed and said to his servants, "Can we find anyone like this man, one in whom is the spirit of God?" (41:38).

Even when Joseph was abused and forgotten, God's favor opened the next chapter in his life. When he suffered injustice or when he was pushed to the margins, it was God's favor that gave him access to those in power. Even though God's favor did *not* always protect him from the harm and neglect of others who sometimes wished him evil, it always overrode their intentions. Even when God's favor didn't keep these things from happening, there was an opposite and equal response to whatever Joseph's enemies had planned.

By the time Joseph arrived in his new position as second in command only to the pharaoh himself, he was still in his thirties (41:41–43, 46). But Joseph already knew how he got there: "It is because God has made me fruitful in the land of my suffering" (41:52). Nearly ten years later, when a famine destroyed the will and the reserves of everyone in the region, Joseph's brothers were forced to journey to Egypt so they could beg for food. Who should they run into, but Joseph himself!

"I am your brother," he said, "the one you sold into Egypt! . . . Do not be angry with yourselves for selling me here, because it was to save lives that God sent me on ahead of you . . . to preserve for you a remnant on earth and to save your lives by a great deliverance" (45:4–5, 7).

Like the stewards in Jesus' parable of the talents, Joseph did not view his success as something he earned. It wasn't his hard work, clever ideas, or dumb luck. It was something God had entrusted to him because God was trying to accomplish something with Joseph's entire family. God was slowly turning the solitary figure of Jacob (Joseph's father) into the twelve tribes of Israel, and there was a famine in the way. So God shared his power with Joseph in hopes that Joseph would put it to work until his master returned. And what exactly did Joseph do with this power? His conversation with his brothers provides an important clue. Perhaps it's a model for handling good fortune when it happens to us. Rather than looking at his good fortune and asking, "How can I get more?" or even, "How do I keep from losing it?" Joseph looked at the people who were *behind him*, from whence he had come ("I am your brother, the one you sold into Egypt"). Then he looked *around him* at those he was currently responsible for ("It was to save lives that God sent me on ahead of you"), and these were not just his brothers, but the rest of Egypt too. He knew he must accomplish with this generation what he was sent to accomplish. Then Joseph looked *ahead of him* and saw the bigger picture, and he saw himself as filling an important role in the future ("God sent me ahead of you to preserve for you a remnant on earth"). Joseph knew he must put the past behind him. He was part of the future. Like Jack Whittaker, he had come suddenly into privilege and power, but it was not his own property. It belonged to those who would live ahead of him. Whatever he enjoyed—and enjoy it he would—it was not because he had earned it, but because it was assigned to him, so that he could enjoy the master's happiness while doing the master's work.

Let's look at those three directions again and think about how we may use the favor God has given us.

LOOKING BEHIND US

When we run into good fortune, our first obligation is to those who have the least. Repeatedly we are told to share what we have with those who have less, and this is not so much an obligation as it is an opportunity to share in the master's happiness. This is surely part of his work: "He raises the poor from the dust and lifts the needy from the ash heap; he seats them with princes and has them inherit a throne of honor" (1 Sam. 2:8). And he calls us into this work: "Defend the weak and the fatherless; uphold the cause of the poor and the oppressed. Rescue the weak and the needy; deliver them from the hand of the wicked" (Ps. 82:3–4). In fact, when Mary was first told of the child she would carry in her womb, this is how she imagined him to be: He "has lifted up the humble; he has filled the hungry with good things" (Luke 1:52–53).

Who are the people most affected by the famine? They live careful, industrious lives but have been deprived of power. They are undervalued. Underemployed. They work, whenever they can, but they do not make enough to survive. They are underpaid. Overlooked. Stuck in the caste system. We do the master's work when we help establish them, employ them, honor them, and give them access to power. Sometimes they are the ones who carried us — teachers, mentors, coaches, parents, and friends — but just as often they are strangers. Always they are victims of an ill fate they did not cause but have fallen into.

LOOKING AROUND US

Who has God entrusted to our care? Who are we responsible for? And how does our fortune put us in a position to help them? What are we able to do now that we were not able to do before? When we look around us, we're looking for someone to believe in, someone to sponsor. Sometimes this can mean money, but just as often it can mean our social capital. As we become more and more successful, we often move into social networks that are more powerful and affluent. We get invited into circles that are more prominent in the community. Suddenly we are no longer six degrees from Kevin Bacon; we are only four—then two—and before long we have Kevin Bacon's number on our cell phone. As God moves us into different spheres, we must share our access with others who need it.

In my denomination, the General Superintendent is a senior executive who has spent years cultivating these connections. Her work is well-known by leaders across the church and in governments around the world. Jo Anne Lyon has worked tirelessly to develop economic trusts in Africa, to end sex trafficking in Eastern Europe, to build medical clinics and schools in the world's poorest countries. Her work has brought her into the company of presidents and heads of state. But Jo Anne knows that this is not her own doing, and it's not forever. She will not always have the kind of favor she has today, and I've heard her say on several occasions that her chief concern now is to introduce others from this tiny denomination to great leaders around the world. Jo Anne is sharing her social capital with others who do the Master's work.

As always, we have to be careful to spend our favor on those who have character, who are ambitious and unselfish, who will not use it on themselves. We have to seek people with vision, who are able to multiply what we give them to create even more opportunities, people who are in a position to one day influence hundreds of others.

LOOKING AHEAD OF US

Joseph said, "God sent me ahead of you to preserve for you a remnant." In other words, God was doing something bigger than whatever was happening in that little moment. He was saving not just a family but a whole remnant from the famine, so that he could weave it into a new nation some years down the road. God was saving not just Joseph and his brothers but their descendants, whom they would never meet. Joseph's success was a crucial link between a tribe and a nation. Of course, Joseph himself would not be there, but his work, and the favor he received from God, would be the platform upon which a new nation would rise.

Like Joseph, we have an obligation to those who come after us. Whenever we find favor with God, we must remember that it is not all about us. God is doing something *now* with us, to set himself up for what he will do *later*, after we are gone. Most of the time we cannot know exactly what that is. But we can ask the right questions.

In my church, I believe we've seen God's favor for at least the last seven or eight years. We've seen our little congregation grow and change into things we only imagined a few years ago and we have backed into most of it. We are becoming a church that is intergenerational, intercultural, and diverse. We have a higher profile in our community and a stronger voice in our denomination. We are beginning to reach not only the lost, but the very lost. In the past few years, we have developed new ministries in public schools, the hardest neighborhoods, strip clubs, and prisons; and we are seeing some incredible conversions take place. But I cannot help but wonder what might come next. In spite of how much fun we're having now, I can't help but wonder what God really has in mind some years down the road, for which he needs us to manage this favor in the present day. What things does our work make possible for the future? Given our trajectory, or how far we have come, and given the kind of people that God is assembling in our community, what could we become for the city and for the kingdom some years down the road? What pitfalls should we avoid? What opportunities should we seize? I cannot know exactly what God has in mind, but I can get pretty excited about it and I can bring together the right people to help answer these questions.

What might God be doing in your family, business, or neighborhood for which you are a crucial link? Try to imagine your family or church twenty or even fifty years from now. What could they do together for the kingdom of God? And what might they need from you now?

TALKING DUTCH

Some years ago when I pastored a church in Michigan, I asked my friend Bud Bence to come up for a weekend and speak to our leaders. One morning, he decided to walk the shores of Lake Huron so he could think and pray before addressing the leaders later that morning. Before he knew it, Bud had wandered off the public access and onto the property of a landowner who was private . . . and watching.

"Hey, what are you doing on my property?" he shouted from the porch. Bud apologized and explained he didn't mean to interrupt, that he was from out of town and that he was taking some time to pray while enjoying the sunrise. But the landowner was not impressed.

"You don't belong on this property," he said. "This is my property and if you want to do that you have to go down there, to the public access."

Once more Bud apologized, only this time with a point that was lost on the landowner, "I'm sorry. . . . I didn't mean to steal your sunrise."

"Well, go on then and get outta here," he said with the wave of his hand.

Bud and I have laughed about that ever since.

What do you say to a man who thinks he owns the sunrise? How do you tell him that he will not have less of his property or his sunrise if he shares it with you? How do you convince him that there will be another tomorrow that he didn't earn and that he can share as much of it as he likes without ever running out? Now think about your own sunrise.

What has God given you that you do not deserve? What would you do with it if you knew he would replace it with more tomorrow? Many times we protect our authority, intellectual property, status, or social connections as if it were our sunrise. We get nervous when others wander too close to our possessions or ideas without quoting us or asking for permission. Are we afraid that they will diminish? Do we think we'll run out? Those who give liberally to things the Master is doing are the freest people in the world. They are part of the new economy, in which people are measured, not by what they possess, but by what they give away. They have laid up their treasure in heaven and their hearts have followed. And what do they get in exchange?

Like Joseph, even after they are gone their descendants will carry them along into the future that they helped to make possible. Then, together with those they have never met, God will make them perfect (Heb. 11:40).

8

A DEATH

finding our heart's true home

There was once a landowner who sent his servant into Baghdad to do some business. A few hours later, the servant returned in a panic.

"What happened?" asked the landowner.

"I was halfway through your business," said the servant, "when I came face to face with Death. He threatened me with a look like I have never seen. Please, sir, give me a loan and give me your fastest horse. I must ride like fury into Samarra, where Death cannot find me, and there I will be safe."

So the landowner granted the servant his wish, and then he mounted his own horse and rode into town himself to confront Death. When he found him, he asked, "Why did you frighten my servant? Why did you give him a threatening look?"

"I don't know what you're talking about," said Death. "I didn't give your servant a threatening look. I was only surprised to see him here in Baghdad, for I have an appointment with him tomorrow . . . in Samarra."[1]

Of all the Faultlines, the one we avoid the most is death. But oddly enough, it is the one FaultLine we will all be on at one time or another. We know very little about it.

Those who talk about death have never died, and those who have died aren't talking. The same is true of heaven. The theologians who know so much about it have never been, and the ones who have been aren't telling us anything. So most of the time, when we speak of it, we talk in terms of what it isn't—no suffering, no crying—but the closer we get to going there, the more we wonder, "What is it, really?" I have sat with the dying in dark rooms or knelt next to their beds; I have read them the Scriptures or sung to them their favorite songs. The heaviness in the room is palpable. But so is the joy. The moment is full of beauty and violence, triumph and sadness, hope and despair. This is sacred space.

Here the soul is shouting like at no other time. Those who are dying, no matter how triumphant they sound, have questions they cannot ask. Not here. Not now. It seems too late. They're like a first-time skydiver, pausing just before the leap, wondering what he has gotten himself into. Will the parachute open? Will he land safely? Of course, you always do, right? But what if he's wrong? What if there's something he overlooked, something crucial, something he should have done? More than any other event, death causes great anxiety.

Most of us do not think of ourselves dying. Even though we know we'll die someday, there's very little about life that prepares us for dying. Then, all at once, it is upon us.

As a young pastor, I was called to the home of a middle-aged man who had just been released from the hospital with the grim news that he had only six weeks to live. When I arrived he was sitting in the living room, still wearing the wrist band, staring out the window. Everything I asked, he deflected. He never said more than two words at a time.

Was he afraid? "Nope!"

What was he feeling? "Not much."

Was he prepared? "I guess."

The whole time he never looked at me.

Would he mind if I prayed? "Go ahead," he said.

So I prayed, then I left. All the way home I kicked myself for not asking better questions. But I couldn't. I was as lost as he was. What would he do? What would I do? Indeed, what does anyone do on the day he hears he has only six weeks to live? It was like he had crossed a boundary that separates those who are alive from those who are dying. That boundary is like a Faultline.

TWO WAYS OF DYING

Like every FaultLine, the prospect of dying exaggerates our condition, whatever it is. It amplifies our tendencies, making us better saints or sinners.

This is nowhere more evident than on Good Friday. According to Luke, two others were crucified with Jesus that day—one on each side of him—and between them was a world of difference.

"One of the criminals who hung there hurled insults at him: 'Aren't you the Messiah? Save yourself and us!' But the other criminal rebuked him. 'Don't you fear God,' he said. . . . 'We are punished justly, for we are getting what our deeds deserve. But this man has done nothing wrong.' Then he said, 'Jesus, remember me when you come into your kingdom.' Jesus answered him, 'Truly I tell you, today you will be with me in paradise'" (Luke 23:39–43).

Interestingly, both men were called criminals. Both heard the prayer, "Father, forgive them." Both would die within the hour. But from there, the FaultLine of death moved them in opposite directions. Let's compare. One was desperate; the other was at peace. One was becoming less religious (he "blasphemed"); the other was becoming more religious (he "feared God"). One had aligned himself with the world that was deriding Jesus ("Aren't you the Messiah?"); the other was aligning himself with Jesus ("This man has done nothing wrong"). One was trying to avoid death ("Save yourself and us"); the other had, in a sense, already died ("Remember me . . . in your kingdom"). One was hoping to be saved from death; the other was hoping to be saved through death. One was holding on; the other was letting go. And all of this was happening in a few hours. Death was a FaultLine that separated not only the characters of these men, but also their destinies. One asked to be saved and was afterward forgotten; the other asked only to be remembered and was saved.

This FaultLine runs through every human soul. Those who try to avoid death are ruined. Those who embrace it are saved. Hard as it is, we must learn to reconcile with our death. But like the servant who ran to Samarra, we try to avoid death even while we move toward it.

THE CULT OF DEATH AVOIDANCE

Those who want to avoid death use different methods. Some minimize it in superficial terms, as though it were overrated. Just yesterday I read the obituary of a man who died prematurely at sixty-four years old that said he "went to heaven to go fishing with his brother Gene and brother-in-law Rex." Anyone who took that statement seriously would think that dying was just the sending off to an extended vacation. One woman told me that her husband was there "cheering for the Yankees." But if he was cheering for the Yankees, I wondered, what on earth was he doing in heaven? Wouldn't he really be in . . . well, I didn't ask.

A bit more serious are those who deny death. With the rise of science and technology, there's been an unbridled optimism about living forever. *Time* magazine recently reported on scientists' attempts to conquer death: "Old age is an illness like any other. And what do you do with illnesses? You cure them!" It sounds funny, I know, but they insist "there's actual science going on here."[2] In fact, researchers at Harvard Medical School recently administered a new drug to a group of mice who were experiencing age-related diseases, and do you know what happened? "The mice didn't just get better; they got younger."[3]

There are real possibilities here. Now the secret is to stay alive long enough to figure out how not to die. And how long will that take? Some say it will be here as soon as 2045. If you're already over sixty, you were probably born too early to live forever. "Modern medicine struggles with dying," writes Carol Zaleski, a Harvard grad herself, "not because it is painful—it has always been painful—but because it signals the failure of our technology."[4]

We are living in a culture that avoids death. Even among Christians, the memorial service has replaced the traditional funeral, often with the body not present. A private disposition of the body has already taken place so that no one will have to confront the lifeless. A brief, simple, and highly personalized homily focuses on the deceased with little mention of the plain fact that they have died. It's like this is their fifteen minutes. Such changes would not seem significant except that, as Thomas Long has noted, "Our theology shapes our funeral practices and vice versa. A change in our practice signals a commensurate shift in our theology." As our funeral practices change, it means that "something about how we view death theologically is changing as well."[5]

When we enter the valley of the shadow of death, we are on a FaultLine. We must not squander this season by avoiding it. We have work to do here, and we cannot cram all of it into the last few hours. We must not wait until we have but six weeks to live. "It is important to face death before we are in any real danger of dying," writes Henri Nouwen. "If we start thinking about death when we are terminally ill, our reflections will not be deep enough and will not give us the support we need as death draws near. As the German mystic, Jacob Boehme said, 'He who dies not before he dies, is ruined when he dies.'"[6]

As often as I have walked with people on this FaultLine, I have not always done it well. Only recently has it occurred to me that most of our efforts as ministers are put into stabilizing the family and not into shepherding those who are actually dying. Most of our conversations with the dying are about heaven—as though we knew what we were talking about—and not about the art of dying well. We talk about what they did in the past or about what they want for their funeral. But what about their questions? Their fears? Their confessions? Their unfinished business? Most of our counseling is merely listening, and whatever they say, if it's really good, is sure to make it into our homily at the funeral. But what are we doing to actually help the dying prepare? The physicians can tell them what will happen to their bodies. But can we tell them what will happen to their souls? Can we tell them what to expect? Do we know? Have we contemplated what changes await them internally? And can we help them move through those changes? I have become pretty good at doing funerals. I know how to memorialize the dead. But do I know how to help with the dying? These questions plague me, even after thirty years, because I need to do a better job. I need to learn how to be a priest again.

LIVING LIKE WE'RE DYING

The dying have lots of questions. The most common refer to life after death. What will it be like when they first open their eyes in the new world? Will they see their loved ones? And will they know them? But I don't think these are the questions their souls are really asking. The real struggle is not between heaven and hell but between heaven and earth.

Sometimes, the night before I travel, I will sit on my bed with my suitcase half packed and stare out the window wondering why I agreed to travel. I am busy enough at home. I have friends and routines, and I have my family whom I love very much, so I have no need to travel if I can't them take them with me. But invariably, as I drive to the airport and wait for my plane, I grow a little more distant from home. I start to think about my engagement on the road. I think about the people I'll meet and how packed my schedule will be for the next three days. The airport can be a necessary buffer between home and life on the road, so that by the time I arrive at my engagement I am not missing my family at all. I get enthralled in my new life out there on the road. I meet new people, and as I listen to their stories and talk about their churches, I make new friends. At first, my wife used to wonder why I didn't call every night, but now she knows that I'm absentminded on the road. I'm embarrassed to say it, but sometimes I get so lost in my work on the road that I completely forget I have a home. But eventually my responsibilities there wind down, and as they do I start thinking of home. On the last night, I'll say good-bye to my new friends and head back to my room. I'll sit on the bed with my suitcase half packed and stare out the window thinking of home. In the morning I will head for the airport, which again will be a necessary buffer between my life on the road and my home. I'll get a call from my wife, and a text message from the office saying, "Yay . . . you get to come home." And from the moment my plane leaves that city to the moment I walk through the door, all I can think about is home.

This is what happens to the soul on the FaultLine of dying. It's trying to detach itself from life on the road and reorient itself toward home. The season of dying is like sitting in the airport, awaiting our flight. It is a necessary buffer between life on the road and home. But there is important work to do while we are waiting. What follows are some of the significant changes I've seen in the saints God has entrusted to my care while they wait in the airport.

DISENTANGLEMENT: FROM HOLDING ON TO LETTING GO

The first thing we must do is to slowly disentangle from the world. When we disentangle, we let go of our attachments. We lose our taste for things. Writing to the president of France, who was nervous at the prospect of dying, Saint Francis de Sales chided him, saying, "We must leisurely say good-bye to the world and little by little withdraw our affections from [it]." He compared those who die suddenly to trees that are ripped out of the soil by the wind. They leave their roots in the earth, and so they are not prepared for the place where they are going. "But he who would carry trees into another soil," said Francis, "must skillfully disengage little by little all the roots, one after the other."[7] To let go is to relinquish our attachment to things. It is to de-clutter. To downsize. To live simply on less.

It is common today to consume, and relish what time we have left in this world. The older we get, the more we clutter our houses with memories. Everything is sentimental, which means that as long as we have it we can hold onto the past. We can hardly be faulted for this, but it leaves our families in a bind. They must decide without us which of our things are still valuable and which are pure junk. I have seen families paralyzed by this, even for years, because to throw away what the dying have loved feels like burying them again. As for the dying, they wanted only to be remembered by their loved ones, but the memories that are left have been tainted by things that have entangled them with this world. In the end, those who wanted to bless their families have cursed them. And this happens not only among seniors, but also with the terminally ill in their midlife. And it happens with not only our possessions, but with our positions, control, image, and liberties. When we hold on to them longer than we should, we force the next generation to pry them from us, often with no instructions for how to use them. Everything dying takes from us—every inch of freedom, every ounce of dignity, every sensation of pleasure—we begrudge. Like the criminal who cried, "Save yourself and us too," we have not disentangled from the world.

What the other criminal recognized was that Jesus was "entering his kingdom," but he probably didn't mean heaven, at least not as we think of it today. The "kingdom" into which Jesus was going was a realm or a domain under his influence. My friend, this is the world into which we are going. It is vastly different from the one we are in. It's a world dominated by those who are poor in spirit. The meek are like rock stars, the peacemakers are people of valor, and those persecuted wear their scars like badges of honor. In the land where we're going, a holy person is known by the way she associates with the unholy, and not by the way she avoids them. He is measured by what he gives away, not by what he possesses. It's a place where sovereignty washes a servant's feet, where the untouchable God lets children crawl all over him, where the most powerful ride on donkeys, where the all-knowing stand silent when taunted by their inferiors, where a Savior can save others but he chooses not to save himself. It's a place where to be safe we must put ourselves in jeopardy, to save our lives we lose them, to move up we step down, to be strong we confess our weakness, to be sinless we remain humbly conscious of our sin. It's a place where admitting our foolishness makes us wise, where standing firm is moving forward, where to be comforted we must mourn, and to fight we must get on our knees. When A. W. Tozer wrote of it, he called this paradox "that incredible Christian."[8] And the kingdom of God is full of them.

For this reason, I have said many times—only half-jokingly—that the mission of the church is to seek and save, not only the dying who are going to hell, but those who are going to heaven and won't like it because it is nothing of whatever they like. To let go is to gradually prepare for this world. Perhaps a good place to start is by spending an hour every week, or every day when we are dying, to ask ourselves, "What is the real value of the things I value?" Real wisdom, said one Catholic saint of the past, "consists in the mind's giving to things the importance they have in reality."[9]

DISEMPOWERMENT: FROM A DYING INDIVIDUAL TO A LIVING COMMUNITY

There is a striking scene toward the end of Joseph's life where he called in his brothers to give them his dying wishes. These were the same brothers who once beat him up and left him for dead. Now, ninety-three years later, they gathered as old men around dying Joseph and he had to, once more, trust them. "I am about to die," he said. "But God will surely come to your aid and take you up out of this land [Egypt] to the land that he promised [our fathers]" (Gen. 50:24). What did he want from them? Only one thing: "When you go," he said, "you must carry my bones [with you] up from this place" (50:25).

Joseph made a remarkable transition that would make his dying easier. As we read his last words, our attention is shifted from the one dying to those still alive. The focus has moved subtly from an individual to the community, from Joseph's private death to the larger life of his family. In fact, Joseph's life in Egypt was only his life on the road. It could only be told as part of the larger story God was telling with his people. And so, as his little life came to a close, he humbly placed it in the larger community. His little life, as important as it seemed to him, was only the link between Jacob (his father) and Israel (his descendants).

I have thought about Joseph many times when thinking about my own death. I have wondered, "What was the role of my father in the story God is telling with my family? And what is my role? How does it fit in the story God may be telling over a hundred years?" As a life comes to a close, people's attention is gradually shifted toward the dying person. The family gathers. The minister is summoned. But before entering those hours, I wonder if we could do more to embed our lives into the larger story God is telling. I wonder if we could humbly place ourselves within the larger faith community.

As we come to the end of our lives, it is essential to pass on to others what glory we have gained for ourselves. We must work our way to the back of the line by empowering others who are behind us and moving them into places where they can affect the whole community. One way of doing this is to bless our successors, as all of the patriarchs in the Bible did. We may write it in a letter or say it face-to-face, but however we do it, a blessing usually has a couple of components. It contains something about the recipient that is unique and valuable to the whole community, and it contains a charge to invest those contributions in the kingdom of God.

Somewhere I've read that the greatest fear among the dying is that they will not be remembered. It's not only that they will be absent from the daily lives of their family; it's that somehow—after the family has gotten over the shock—the person's absence will not be noticed. It's the fear that others won't miss them, once they have found other friends or spouses. The natural inclination is thus to keep others, as long as we can, absorbed with our lives. But in our dying, we must learn that others do not belong to us. Rather, we belong to them. The only way to move forward is to have them carry us, as Joseph's brothers carried him, to the place where God is taking us together.

DEVOTION: FROM HEAVEN TO CHRIST

Sometimes I'm embarrassed when I look over the homilies I have given at funerals. Without trying, I have nurtured in them a love for heaven more than a love for Christ. These are not opposite each other, but neither are they the same thing. Heaven is streets of gold. Heaven is being with those we love. Heaven is "fishing with our brother Gene and our brother-in-law Rex." I certainly don't want to undermine any hope we have for the family reunion we're planning for heaven. I have loved ones I want to see too.

But I want to remind us that in the New Testament at least, the emphasis among those who are dying was never on heaven, but on Christ. In fact, I can think of no place in the New Testament where the dying were said to be in the presence of loved ones who preceded them in death. There is no place in which the departed are said to be with anyone—whether grandma or children or even their spouse— even though we have every reason to believe they will. It's not that this idea is wrongheaded; it's just that it isn't the focus of the New Testament.

When the first martyr, Stephen, was dying, he "looked up to heaven and saw . . . *Jesus* standing at the right hand of God" (Acts 7:55, emphasis added). When Paul teetered in between life and death, he knew that "to depart and be *with Christ* . . . is better by far" (Phil. 1:23, emphasis added). When John looked into the heavens, on the island of Patmos, he was consumed with "someone like a *son of man*" (Rev. 1:13, emphasis added). I am concerned about the emphasis that the church has put on heaven to the near exclusion of Jesus Christ. While we are yet dying, we must move our affections first to Christ.

Christ is not just one person in heaven. He is not even the most important person in heaven. He is the whole kingdom of God. He is the new man. He is the image, the kind, the type of person we are becoming. He is the place where God and humanity meet. He is the center of the Christian story, the love of the Father, and the preoccupation of the Holy Spirit. He is the Alpha and Omega, the beginning and end. He is the salvation of our souls. He is the consummate friend, the unfailing advocate, the fellow in our sufferings, the bridegroom at our wedding. Indeed, our lives will not end in God's courtroom with Christ as our defense. They will end in God's sanctuary with Christ as the groom, standing at the end of a long aisle that has been our lives, waiting to initiate our vows, leading us into the presence of the Father and showing us the culture of heaven. This is the witness of the New Testament.

My friend, heaven is not who we think it is. It's not grandpa, mother, or brothers in arms. It is Christ. We simply must develop more desire for him in the FaultLine of dying. The degree to which he does not possess us, to which we desire others more than him, is the degree to which heaven will seem like a strange place. We must learn to desire him. We must come to know him better.

FROM DYING TO COMING ALIVE

It may surprise us, but the New Testament says nothing about life after death for the Christian. This is not just some kind of denial. Throughout history, the people of God have died just as often and sometimes more violently than the people of the world. The difference is that they have never seen it as merely dying, but as coming alive.

There's a powerful little story about this hidden in the Gospels. A fellow named Jairus, who was very religious, had a little girl who was sick. Hearing that Jesus was coming to town, Jairus ventured to find him. Then, falling at Jesus' feet, he begged him, "Please come and put your hands on her so that she will be healed and live" (Mark 5:23). I don't know how many times I have prayed that very thing on behalf of families in my church. Sometimes he does, and sometimes he doesn't. This time he didn't.

By the time Jairus could wrestle Jesus free from the crowd, his servants had come to find him. "'Your daughter is dead,' they said. 'Why bother the teacher anymore?'" (5:35). Can you hear the despair? Why do we keep bothering Jesus when the worst has happened? What does it matter now? Here is where religion hits the wall. We will pray for something so long as it appears it might happen. But when it is clear that things will not end as we had hoped, we don't want to bother him anymore.

But it is here that a very strange thing occurs. From this point on, it seems that Jesus and others were looking at the same thing, only they were seeing it from different sides. One saw it as dying. The other saw it as coming alive. Immediately, Jesus told Jairus, "Just believe" (5:36), and he insisted on going to Jairus's home. By the time he arrived, the mourners had started making a scene.

"Why all this commotion?" said Jesus. "The child is not dead but asleep" (5:39). And then, in one shocking verse, we are told how far removed they were from reality: "They laughed at him" (5:40). Whenever Jesus says something you can hardly believe, it is probably not a good idea to laugh. There is always a very good chance that he knows something you don't. In the Greek, it's even worse. The imperfect tense of the verb suggests that they kept laughing.

"Look, Jesus," they must have said, "you weren't even here when she died. How do you know? We were with her. Her organs have shut down, her breathing has stopped, her complexion has changed, her eyes have closed, her pulse has quit, and there are no brain waves. This, in common parlance, is called death." And they laughed.

Everything they'd said was true . . . except for the diagnosis. Jesus and the others agreed on the symptoms, but they differed on what they all meant. The vital signs were only one way of describing what had happened. There were other ways, and besides, there was more happening than met the eye.

So Jesus excused himself and went into the child's room.

"Little girl," he said, "I say to you, get up!" (5:40). And immediately she got up and started walking around.

TALKING DUTCH

I remember the day I learned this. I have never been the same in the presence of the dying. I was visiting a member who was suffering with cancer at the young age of forty-eight. Every treatment, prayer, and anointing to keep him alive had failed. One Saturday morning, at 5:30, they called and said, "Please come. Gene is dying." When I arrived, the sun was in the distance but rising quickly, casting its warmth across the foot of his bed. I hugged the family. I cited Scripture. We sang songs. We prayed. As I looked around the room, we seemed as desperate as anyone in the world. Then I heard it. A voice from within me asked, "What do you see?" I could not get away from it.

I looked into the face of our dying friend and muttered under my breath, so no one could hear me, "I see our friend slipping away."

"Look again," said the voice. "What do you see?"

"I see loss. I see grief. I see unanswered prayers that have fallen to the ground and died." The more I talked, the more cynical I became. "I see a man who trusted you all his life, lying there getting the life beat out of him by something you could cure, but you won't. That's what I see."

"Look again," said the voice. "Things are not as they seem. What do you see?"

I stepped forward to pray, and within a few moments Gene was gone.

I stayed about a half hour, comforting the family, then excused myself and went back to the office, where I closed the door and came apart. "Aren't you the Messiah?" I prayed. My religion was in crisis. My soul was troubled.

Later that afternoon, as I prepared for the funeral, I stumbled upon Paul's description of dying, and it stopped me in my tracks. "We grow weary in our present bodies," he said, "and we long to put on our heavenly bodies like new clothing. . . . While we live in these earthly bodies, we groan and sigh [because] . . . we want to put on our new bodies so that these dying bodies will be swallowed up by life" (2 Cor. 5:2, 4 NLT).

"Look again," said the voice. "What did you see?"

And I wept.

That tiny bedroom was a FaultLine, and my friend and I were on opposite sides. It was making him better. It was making me worse. He was letting go of one life for another. I was trying to keep him in this one. He was already praying, "Jesus, remember me," and I was praying, "Aren't you the Christ? Save yourself and us too." I thought my friend was dying, but he was coming alive. Like a new-born, he was birthed into a life that is richer, more colorful, and more permanent than anything in this tiny world.

Those who live on the FaultLine of dying are called into this room where they must decide whether to believe or laugh, to let go or hold on. They must choose which reality to cling to. For those who cling to the reality that is Christ, they will find in their dying, as night closes in, they are passing into one unending day.

NOTES

INTRODUCTION

1. John Oswalt, *Called to Be Holy: A Biblical Perspective* (Nappanee, IN: Evangel, 1999), 1.

2. Ibid., 3–4.

3. Jon Meacham, "The End of Christian America," *Newsweek*, April 13, 2009, 34.

4. Ibid., 36.

5. G. K. Chesterton has noted, "In the absence of God, men do not worship nothing; they worship everything."

6. Mark Guaring, "Faith-Mixing Common in U.S.," *The Christian Science Monitor*, January 24, 2010, 20.

7. Kenda Creasy Dean, *Almost Christian: What the Faith of Our Teenagers Is Telling the American Church* (Oxford: Oxford University Press, 2010), 21.

8. Hannah More, *Religion of the Heart* (Orleans, MA: Paraclete, 1993), 40.

9. Steve DeNeff, *The Way of Holiness: Experience God's Work in You* (Indianapolis, IN: Wesleyan Publishing House, 2010), 21.

10. Gordon T. Smith, *Beginning Well: Christian Conversion and Authentic Transformation* (Downers Grove, IL: IVP, 2001), 24.

CHAPTER 1

1. Keith Drury, e-mail message to author, January 14, 2014.
2. Steve DeNeff and David Drury, *SoulShift: The Measure of a Life Transformed* (Indianapolis, IN: Wesleyan Publishing House, 2011), 24–25.
3. Thomas Moore, *Care of the Soul: A Guide for Cultivating Depth and Sacredness in Everyday Life* (New York: HarperCollins, 1992), 5–6.
4. *New International Dictionary of New Testament Theology*, ed. Colin Brown, vol. 3 (Grand Rapids, MI: Zondervan, 1986), 709.
5. Frederick Dale Bruner, *The Gospel of John: A Commentary* (Grand Rapids: Eerdmans, 2012), 726.
6. Brennan Manning, *Ruthless Trust: The Ragamuffin's Path to God* (New York: HarperCollins, 2000), 5.
7. Ibid., 12–13.

CHAPTER 2

1. Oswald Chambers, *Not Knowing Whither the Steps of Abraham Faith* (London: Marshall, Morgan & Scott, 1934), 12.
2. Peggy Post, "Call Waiting Rules," *Good Housekeeping*, accessed June 13, 2014, www.goodhousekeeping.com/family/etiquette/call-waiting- rules-oct01.
3. Dallas Willard, *The Divine Conspiracy: Recovering Our Hidden Life in God* (New York: HarperCollins, 1998), 282.
4. Charles Beckett, "A Life Well Lived," *Triangle Magazine*, Winter 2011, 10.
5. Ibid.

CHAPTER 3

1. *Wikipedia*, s.v. "perfect storm," last modified February 2, 2014, http://en.wikipedia.org/wiki/Perfect_storm.
2. St. John of the Cross, *Dark Night of the Soul*, trans. E. Allison Peers (New York: Doubleday, 1990), 104.
3. Steve DeNeff and David Drury, *SoulShift: The Measure of a Life Transformed* (Indianapolis, IN: Wesleyan Publishing House, 2011), 65.

CHAPTER 4

1. Tessa Stuart, "Opie of 'Opie & Anthony' Smashes Homeless Man's Cake, Doesn't Get Why People Aren't Laughing," *The Village Voice* (blog), August 12, 2013, http://blogs.villagevoice.com/runninscared/2013/08/opie_of_opie_an.php.
2. "Homeless Andrew AFTER 2007 Cake stomp—@OpieRadio," YouTube video, 3:14, posted by "Opie Radio," August 16, 2013, https://www.youtube.com/watch?v=IAu2Q1I9lOM.
3. Randy Hodson, *Dignity at Work* (Cambridge: Cambridge University Press, 2001), 5–13.
4. Robert Alter, *The Five Books of Moses: A Translation with Commentary* (New York: W. W. Norton & Company, 2004), 78.
5. Oswald Chambers, *Not Knowing Whither the Steps of Abraham Faith* (London: Marshall, Morgan & Scott, 1934), 47.

6. Watchman Nee, *Sit, Walk, Stand* (Fort Washington, PA: Christian Literature Crusade, 1966), 25–26.

CHAPTER 5

1. David Rock, *Your Brain at Work: Strategies for Overcoming Distraction, Regaining Focus, and Working Smarter* (New York: HarperCollins, 2009), 48.
2. Ibid., 55.
3. Colkoch, "Sins and the Sexes," *Enlightened Catholicism* (blog), February 18, 2009, http://enlightenedcatholicism-colkoch.blogspot.com/2009/02/sins-and-sexes.html.
4. Earl Woods, with Fred Mitchell, *Playing Through: Straight Talk on Hard Work, Big Dreams, and Adventures with Tiger* (New York: HarperCollins, 1998), 83–84.
5. C. S. Lewis, *The Weight of Glory* (Grand Rapids, MI: Eerdmans, 1966), 2–3.

CHAPTER 6

1. Jason Beck, "Missed Call Ends Galarraga's Perfect Bid," MLB.com, June 3, 2010, http://mlb.mlb.com/news/article.jsp?ymd=20100602&content_id=10727590.
2. Tom Verducci, with Melissa Segura, "A Different Kind of Perfect," *Sports Illustrated*, June 14, 2010, 46.
3. Ibid.
4. Melinda Beck, "Inside the Minds of the Perfectionists," *The Wall Street Journal*, October 30, 2012, D4.
5. Verducci, "A Different Kind of Perfect," 46.
6. Leonard Mlodinow, *Subliminal: How Your Unconscious Mind Rules Your Behavior* (New York: Random House, 2012), 198.
7. Hannah More, *Religion of the Heart* (Orleans, MA: Paraclete, 1993), 122.
8. Reinier Schippers, *Dictionary of New Testament Theology*, ed. Colin Brown, vol. 3 (Grand Rapids, MI: Zondervan, 1986), 351.

CHAPTER 7

1. "Lottery Curse," YouTube video, from ABC News interview, posted by "Unplugged Boy," April 26, 2010, http://www.youtube.com/watch?v=RPGzo6LkfuA.
2. "Adversity," Bartleby.com, accessed June 13, 2014, http://www.bartleby.com/348/36.html.
3. Graeme Wood, "The Fortunate Ones," *The Atlantic*, April 2011, 76.
4. Ibid., 77–78.
5. Tim Kasser, *The High Price of Materialism* (Cambridge, MA: MIT Press, 2002), 16–17.
6. Robert Frank, "Will Winning the Lottery Ruin Your Life?" *The Wealth Report* (blog), *The Wall Street Journal*, March 30, 2012, http://blogs.wsj.com/wealth/2012/03/30/will-winning-the-lottery-ruin-your-life/.
7. Ibid.

8. Justin Harp, "Roger Waters on Pink Floyd's Breakup: 'Success Ruined Us,'" *Music News* (blog), Digital Spy, January 19, 2012, http://www.digitalspy.com/music/news/a361055/roger-waters-on-pink-floyds-break-up-success-ruined-us.html#~oGrY-BXhaWnnQM5.

9. Joseph A. Fitzmyer, *The Gospel According to Luke*, X–XXIV, The Anchor Bible Commentary (Garden City, NJ: Doubleday & Company, 1983), 1235.

10. Kenneth E. Bailey, *Jesus through Middle Eastern Eyes: Cultural Studies in the Gospels* (Downers Grove, IL: IVP Academic, 2008), 402.

11. Craig S. Keener, *The Bible Background Commentary: New Testament* (Downers Grove, IL: IVP, 1993), 117.

12. Gordon MacDonald, *Ordering Your Private World* (Nashville: Thomas Nelson, 1985), 53.

CHAPTER 8

1. Cited in Charles Swindoll, *Growing Deep in the Christian Life: Essential Truths for Becoming Strong in the Faith* (Grand Rapids, MI: Zondervan, 1995), 300.

2. Lev Grossman, "Singularity," *TIME* magazine, February 21, 2011, 46.

3. Ibid., 47.

4. Carol Zaleski, *The Life of the World to Come: Near-Death Experiences and Christian Hope* (New York: Oxford University Press, 1996), 8.

5. Thomas Long, *Accompany Them with Singing: The Christian Funeral* (Louisville: Westminster John Knox, 2009), 7.

6. Henri Nouwen, with Michael Christensen and Rebecca Laird, *Spiritual Formation: Wisdom for the Long Walk of Faith* (New York: HarperCollins, 2010), 105.

7. Francis de Sales, *Thy Will Be Done: Letters to Persons in the World* (Manchester: Sophia Institute Press, 1995), 112.

8. A. W. Tozer, *That Incredible Christian: How Heaven's Children Live on Earth* (Harrisburg: Christian Publications, 1964), 13.

9. Brennan Manning, *The Importance of Being Foolish: How to Think Like Jesus* (New York: HarperSanFrancisco, 2005), 13.

God's Spirit powerfully flows through His church when it's broken open.

Soul-growing transformation happens to God's people only as he breaks through any spiritual hardness in his church's heart. This powerful church-wide resource provides leadership all they need for an eight-week journey into deeper spiritual formation. Kit contains:

- *FaultLines*—Steve DeNeff reveals to both the young and veteran in faith how soul-growing transformations happen only as God breaks through spiritual hardness.

- Sermon Introductions DVD-ROM—eight engaging video shorts for worship service illustration or introduction. Also an additional FaultLines teaser for promoting the whole series.

- Group Study DVDs—eight twenty-minute videos corresponding with each theme. Author Steve DeNeff, along with other spiritual-formation interviewees, challenge and lead adults of all ages through accessibly paced, transformative group fellowship.

- Online downloadable resources for promoting, organizing, teaching, and preaching.

FaultLines Church Resource Kit
ISBN: 978-0-89827-928-3
Available January 2015

The Measure of a Life Transformed

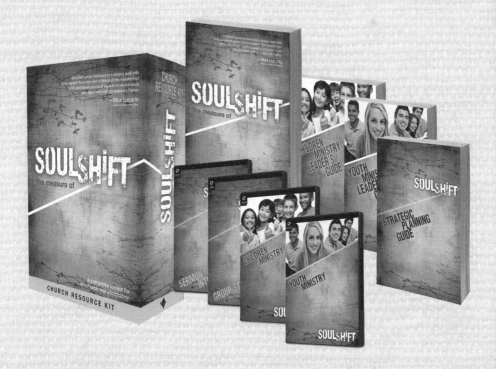

The *SoulShift Church Resource Kit* is an eight-week, church-wide journey that challenges your congregation to experience seven key shifts—life changes that God's Spirit will bring in people's hearts, minds, and behaviors, from the very youngest to the most mature of disciples.

The Kit contains everything your ministry's leadership needs to create a setting for an all-church transformation experience. Use these tools and watch God shift his family—young and old, in the church and in the home—toward the deeper, Spirit-driven life that he desires for his people.

Packed with church-originated and church-tested resources, this kit contains:

- 1 *SoulShift* book
- 1 *Strategic Planning Guide*
- 1 Group Study DVD (3 Discs)
- 1 Sermon Introductions DVD-ROM
- 1 *Youth Ministry Leader's Guide*
- 1 Youth Ministry DVD-ROM
- 1 *Children Ministry Leader's Guide*
- 1 Children Ministry DVD-ROM
- Free online access to SoulShift resources for download

SoulShift Church Resource Kit
ISBN: 978-0-89827-974-0
Available January 2015

Additional Resources from Steve DeNeff

SoulShift: The Measure of a Life Transformed
In *SoulShift*, Steve DeNeff and David Drury offer an approach to spiritual transformation which focuses less on measuring how much time we are spending on spiritual inputs—such as Bible study and prayer—and more on measuring who we are becoming in Christ.

ISBN: 978-0-89827-697-8 | eBook ISBN: 978-0-89827-599-5

7 Saving Graces: Living Above the Deadly Sins
Steve DeNeff unlocks the seven secrets to a life filled with purpose, contentment, and a strong sense of well-being. Keying on the seven most common spiritual problems that we all face—the seven deadly sins—DeNeff points the way toward life transformation by embracing the virtue-filled life of the Spirit.

ISBN: 978-0-89827-420-2 | eBook ISBN: 978-0-89827-685-5

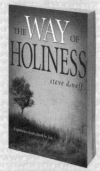

The Way of Holiness: Experience God's Work in You
Steve DeNeff guides you to a full understanding of life as Jesus intended. Along the way, he exposes false assumptions and detours to holiness, examines stages of spiritual growth and decisions in holiness, and encourages living an authentic and practical life of holiness.

ISBN: 978-0-89827-421-9 | eBook ISBN: 978-0-89827-687-9

More Than Forgiveness: Following Jesus into the Heart of Holiness
Too often Christians have thought that obtaining forgiveness from God for our sins was the whole point. Instead, it is the prerequisite for a whole new way of life—the life that God intended when he first placed Adam and Eve in the garden.

ISBN: 978-0-89827-244-4 | eBook ISBN: 978-0-89827-681-7